# BRIGHT YOUNG ROYALS

## Your Guide to the Next Generation of Blue Bloods

### JERRAMY FINE

BERKLEY BOOKS, NEW YORK

THE BERKLEY PUBLISHING GROUP
Published by the Penguin Group
Penguin Group (USA) Inc.
375 Hudson Street, New York, New York 10014, USA
Penguin Group (Canada), 90 Eglinton Avenue East, Suite 700, Toronto, Ontario M4P 2Y3, Canada
(a division of Pearson Penguin Canada Inc.)
Penguin Books Ltd., 80 Strand, London WC2R 0RL, England
Penguin Group Ireland, 25 St. Stephen's Green, Dublin 2, Ireland (a division of Penguin Books Ltd.)
Penguin Group (Australia), 250 Camberwell Road, Camberwell, Victoria 3124, Australia
(a division of Pearson Australia Group Pty. Ltd.)
Penguin Books India Pvt. Ltd., 11 Community Centre, Panchsheel Park, New Delhi—110 017, India
Penguin Group (NZ), 67 Apollo Drive, Rosedale, Auckland, 0632, New Zealand
(a division of Pearson New Zealand Ltd.)
Penguin Books (South Africa) (Pty.) Ltd., 24 Sturdee Avenue, Rosebank, Johannesburg 2196,
South Africa

Penguin Books Ltd., Registered Offices: 80 Strand, London WC2R 0RL, England

The publisher does not have any control over and does not assume any responsibility for author or third-party websites or their content.

BRIGHT YOUNG ROYALS

Copyright © 2011 by Jerramy Fine
Photo credits are listed on page 266
Book design by Tiffany Estreicher

PRINTING HISTORY
Berkley trade paperback edition / October 2011

ISBN: 978-0-425-24687-0

PRINTED IN THE UNITED STATES OF AMERICA

10  9  8  7  6  5  4  3  2  1

# CONTENTS

*For everyone who believes in the magic of royal kingdoms*
*and the promise of happily ever after*

# YOUNG, HOT, & ROYAL

*O*n the dawn of a new millennium, many see monarchies as archaic institutions—as out-of-date and dreary as the castles they inhabit. Some sovereigns, like Queen Elizabeth II, are deeply respected. But many of the older royals, who once upon a time appeared so glamorous, have begun to seem conventional and dull—and thoroughly at odds with the fast, glittering pace of modern life.

Enter the next generation of royal blood! Not only do they glow with the beauty of youth and privilege, but they are stylish, sophisticated, worldly-wise and media-savvy. Most important, almost all are using their royal heritage for something infinitely nobler. Their academic achievements and altruistic track records demonstrate that these princes and princesses possess the character and strength to fulfill their royal duties in ways that have yet to be seen.

Prince William and his glamorous new wife, Catherine Middleton, are the sparkling poster children for this new regal generation. They're good-looking, educated twentysomethings, and for all the media fanfare surrounding their fairy-tale romance, they remain extremely down-to-earth. Unlike so many of the royal couples before them, their nuptials weren't prearranged by the royal establishment. Instead, Will and Kate met in college (like normal people!), and although they hail from vastly different backgrounds, they share the same values and dedication to the greater good. In fact, before meeting at St. Andrews University, they missed bumping into each other by mere months when they both volunteered for the same charity in South America!

When the couple gave their first television interview following the news of their engagement, the relaxed, playful love between them was there for all to see. Many thought Kate would be nervous, but she was charming, gracious, and as ever, stunningly beautiful. Every little girl dreams of meeting Prince Charming; it's heart-warming to watch a girl like Kate actually living the fairy tale.

Like so many of these bright young bluebloods, Kate and William demonstrate fantastic style, a tireless commitment to a gamut of charity causes, and a fierce loyalty to each other, their families, and their country. The following pages contain the hippest, best-looking crowd Europe's monarchies have ever produced. Read on to discover who's who of the young and titled—and see for yourself why these bluebloods are so red hot!

# HRH PRINCE WILLIAM, DUKE OF CAMBRIDGE

**BORN:** June 21, 1982

**ROYAL HERITAGE:** Second in line to the British throne, his parents are HRH Prince Charles and the late Diana, Princess of Wales. His grandmother is HM Queen Elizabeth II.

**EDUCATION:** Eton College; University of St. Andrews (where he studied art history and then geography); Sandhurst Military Academy.

**MILITARY SERVICE:** Lieutenant in the Household Cavalry; also training to be a search-and-rescue pilot with the Royal Air Force.

**WHAT MAKES HIM HOT:** A blond, blue-eyed future king with his father's sense of duty and his mother's sense of compassion. What's not to love?

Those close to William say he is genuine, accessible, levelheaded, and a deep thinker—all good qualities for a modern monarch-to-be. Like Diana, William has a strong philanthropic drive and an easy, unpretentious manner—he is very much the "People's Prince."

**LOVE LIFE:** After years of speculation, royal watchers around the world rejoiced when Prince William's engagement to the glamorously demure Kate Middleton was finally announced on November 16, 2010. William had been dating Kate (his former college flatmate) since 2003, and proposed to her during their recent vacation in Kenya. In an extremely moving gesture, William gave his future bride Princess Diana's sapphire engagement ring to honor his late mother's memory. The glowing young couple married at Westminster Abbey on April 29, 2011, in what all have hailed as the regal event of the century.

**ACTIVITIES**: Polo, rugby, water polo, tennis, swimming, hockey, clay-pigeon shooting, photography. He is also president of the British Academy of Film and Television Arts (BAFTA) as well as president of the Royal Marsden Hospital, a position previously held by his mother.

**MOST LIKELY TO BE FOUND**: At his father's home in Gloucestershire; at Clarence House in London; relaxing on the island of Mustique; skiing in Klosters or Courchevel; enjoying a simple pizza with his wife at his new marital home in North Wales.

**QUOTE**: "All of us, whatever path our lives have taken, are ultimately neighbors and share a common bond."[1]

## PRINCE WILLIAM'S CHARITIES:

◆ *Centrepoint* Provides emergency accommodation, support, information, and training for homeless young people in London. Prince William is a patron. (His mother was also a patron at the time of her death.) William is heavily involved in the charity and recently spent a night sleeping on the streets of London to help raise awareness. http://www.centrepoint.org.uk/

◆ *Henry van Straubenzee Memorial Fund* Aims to lift Ugandan children out of poverty through education. Princes William and Harry are joint patrons. http://www.henryvanstraubenzeemf.org.uk/

◆ *The Child Bereavement Charity* Provides specialized support, information, and training to all those affected when a child or parent dies. Prince William, who knows all too well what it's like to lose a mother, is a patron and often holds private meetings with bereaved families and children supported by the charity. http://www.child bereavement.org.uk

◆ *Tusk Trust* Funds environmental conservation across Africa, combining the interests of people and wildlife alike. Prince William is a patron. http://www.tusk.org/

◆ *The Diana, Princess of Wales Memorial Fund* Established in September 1997 to continue the princess's humanitarian work throughout the world. http://www.theworkcontinues.org/

◆ *The Prince's Rainforests Project* Founded by his father, The Prince of Wales, to discourage deforestation rates and show the vital link between rain forests and climate change. Princes William and Harry appeared alongside their father and an animated frog in a recent public awareness film. http://www.rainforestsos.org

◆ *Raleigh International* A UK-based educational development charity that aims to help people of all backgrounds and nationalities to discover their full potential. Both Prince William and Kate Middleton are Raleigh alumni—Prince William went to Chile with Raleigh International in 2000 and Kate did the same in 2001. http://www.raleighinternational.org/

◆ *The American Friends of the Foundation of Prince William and Prince Harry* Supports the UK Foundation of Prince William and Prince Harry and other charities that support at-risk youth, environmental conservation and injured armed forces. In July 2011, during his North American tour, Prince William played in his first ever American polo match at the Santa Barbara Polo & Racquet Club to raise funds for this charity. http://www.foundationpolochallenge .com/foundation.html

# HRH PRINCESS BEATRICE OF YORK

**BORN:** August 8, 1988

**ROYAL HERITAGE:** Fifth in line to the British throne, her parents are Prince Andrew, the Duke of York, and Sarah, the Duchess of York (aka Fergie). Her grandmother is HM Queen Elizabeth II. Her first cousins are the Princes William and Harry.

**WHAT MAKES HER HOT:** Fiery red hair, large eyes, and rather courageous Lady Gaga–like hatwear. As a Windsor woman, Beatrice is outranked only by her grandmother the Queen, the Duchess of Cornwall, and the new Duchess of Cambridge. Beatrice recently landed a cameo role as a lady-in-waiting in the film *The Young Victoria* (which depicted her great-great-great-great-grandmother).

**QUOTE:** "I have been given circumstances that anyone would wish for and I do believe that I must do something good with it."[2]

**EDUCATION:** Studying history at Goldsmith's University, London.

**SUMMER INTERNSHIP:** Public relations department of the UK Foreign and Commonwealth Office.

**LOVE LIFE:** Since 2007, Beatrice has been stepping out with the handsome David Clark, a wealthy young American (and pal of Prince William's) who works for Virgin's space tourism project.

**ACTIVITIES:** Polo, riding, skiing, Rollerblading, golf, singing (she was in the school choir), music (especially James Blunt), old films (like *High Society*), watching TV (*Desperate Housewives* and *The OC* are her favorites).

**MOST LIKELY TO BE FOUND:** In London's elite nightspots (i.e. Public, Mahiki, Boujis, Chinawhite, the Groucho Club), dining at Nobu or Cipriani; the front row of London Fashion Week; in her own apartment at St. James's Palace.

**WHEN YOU MEET HER OUT ON THE TOWN:** Don't curtsey; don't call her HRH. "I don't want any of that," she told *Hello!* magazine, "I'm just Beatrice."

**BEATRICE'S CHARITIES:**

◆ *Springboard for Children* Provides a literacy lifeline for children with learning difficulties in inner city primary schools. (Beatrice recently went public with her dyslexia, so this charity is especially close to her heart.) http://www.springboard.org.uk/

◆ *Children in Crisis* Founded by her mother, the Duchess of York, it aims to improve the lives of children around the world affected by conflict, deprivation, and poverty. Beatrice was their first ever junior ambassador and in helping to raise funds, she became the first ever royal to run a marathon. She recently auctioned her infamous beige hat (worn to Will and Kate's wedding) and donated one hundred percent of the proceeds, earning over $132,000 for the charity. http://www.childrenincrisis.org/

◆ *The Woodland Trust* The UK's leading woodland conservation charity—Beatrice was recently spotted planting trees on their behalf. http://www.woodlandtrust.org.uk/

◆ *The Teenage Cancer Trust* Devoted to improving the lives of teenagers and young adults with cancer. www.teenagecancertrust.org/

◆ *Elephant Family* Works to save the Asian elephant from extinction and abuse. http://www.elephantfamily.org/

◆ *SOS Children's Villages* The world's largest orphan charity operating in 123 countries. www.soschildrensvillages.org.uk/

# ANDREA CASIRAGHI
# OF MONACO

**BORN:** June 8, 1984

**ROYAL HERITAGE:** Second in line to the Monegasque throne after his mother, HRH Caroline, Princess of Hanover and Hereditary Princess of Monaco. His maternal grandmother is Hollywood icon Grace Kelly. Andrea was six years old when his father, Stefano Casiraghi, died in a speedboat accident. His stepfather is HRH Prince Ernst August of Hanover.

**WHAT MAKES HIM HOT:** Chiseled cheekbones, sun-kissed surfer looks, and Hollywood lineage

**EDUCATION:** McGill University in Canada and the American University in Paris

**LANGUAGES:** French, Italian, English, German

**MOST LIKELY TO BE FOUND:** Clubbing in Manhattan or Ibiza, skiing in Austria at St. Moritz or Zurs, sunning in Tuscany, enjoying the Monaco Grand Prix

**ACTIVITIES:** Politics, art, the environment, long-distance running, riding, skiing, guitar, sailing

**LOVE LIFE:** Has been dating elegant Colombian socialite and airline heiress Tatiana Santo Domingo since 2005.

**ANDREA'S CHARITIES:**
◆ *AMADE* Founded in 1963 by his grandmother HSH Princess Grace of Monaco, the charity seeks to promote and protect chil-

dren's rights on an international level. http://www.amade-mondiale
.org/en

◆ *The Motrice Foundation* Supports research and innovation in the
field of cerebral palsy. Andrea is an ambassador for this foundation,
which was started by the father of a classmate with cerebral palsy.
http://eng.lafondationmotrice.org/

# HRH CROWN PRINCESS VICTORIA OF SWEDEN

**BORN:** July 14, 1977

**ROYAL HERITAGE:** She is the eldest of King Carl XVI Gustaf and Queen Silvia's three children.

**WHAT MAKES HER HOT:** Her engaging smile, casual ponytail, relaxed disposition, and the small fact that she is the only female heir-apparent in the world. (Her younger brother, Carl Philip, who traditionally was bound for the throne under rules of primogeniture, lost out when Sweden became the first monarchy to allow the eldest child—male *or* female—to inherit.)

**QUOTE:** "I don't stop focusing on the job with which I've been entrusted."[3]

**EDUCATION:** Political science and history at Yale University; conflict resolution at Uppsala University, the Swedish National Defence College, the Ministry for Foreign Affairs' Diplomat Program.

**INTERNSHIPS:** United Nations in New York, Swedish Embassy in Washington, DC

**LANGUAGES:** English, French, German, Swedish

**ACTIVITIES:** Dogs, horses, walking, painting, gardening, beekeeping, skiing

**ROYAL FRIENDS:** Fellow heir-apparents, Crown Prince Frederik of Denmark and Crown Prince Haakon of Norway

**LOVE LIFE:** Victoria recently married her commoner boyfriend of eight years, Swedish gym owner Daniel Westling. Tears of joy were shed by the couple during a very regal ceremony at Stockholm Cathedral on June 19, 2010—her parents' thirty-fourth wedding anniversary. At the sumptuous reception attended by royals from throughout Europe, Victoria and Daniel danced an adorable wedding waltz—which is now a popular YouTube video. Known for his down-to-earth demeanor and Clark Kent looks, Daniel used to work as Victoria's personal trainer. Since the wedding, he has received the titles of "Prince Daniel" and "Duke of Västergötland."

**MOST LIKELY TO BE FOUND:** Walking her beloved Labrador Jambo; attending the Advisory Council on Foreign Affairs currently headed by her father, King Carl of Sweden (she steps in as a temporary regent when needed); skiing at her chalet in Storlien; gardening at Solliden Palace, her family's island retreat off the southern coast of Sweden.

**VICTORIA'S CHARITIES:**

◆ *The Crown Princess Victoria Fund* Provides leisure and recreational activities for children with functional disabilities or chronic illnesses. Every year, Victoria visits several of the fund's projects. http://svt.se/svt/jsp/Crosslink.jsp?d=94472

◆ *Swedish International Development Cooperation Agency (SIDA)* Organizes the bulk of Sweden's aid to developing countries. In 2005 Victoria studied Swedish aid initiatives on location in Bangladesh and Sri Lanka. http://www.sida.se/English/

◆ Victoria and Daniel have also set up their own wedding foundation, which will combat youth alienation and promote good health. They ask that anyone wishing to give them a wedding gift donate money to their charity instead.

# LORD FREDERICK (FREDDIE) WINDSOR

**BORN:** April 6, 1979

**ROYAL HERITAGE:** His parents are Prince and Princess Michael of Kent; his father is a first cousin of Her Majesty Queen Elizabeth II. He is thirty-seventh in line to the British throne.

**EDUCATION:** Eton College, and later Oxford University, where he studied classics.

**WHAT MAKES HIM HOT:** Piercing green eyes, party-boy reputation, occasional modeling for Burberry, cameo appearance on *American Idol* (Season 10)

**WORKS:** For investment bank J.P. Morgan as a financial analyst and sometimes writes about music for UK society magazine *Tatler*.

**ACTIVITIES:** Piano, soccer, tennis

**LOVE LIFE:** Married British comedy actress Sophie Winkleman on September 12, 2009, in a large society wedding at Hampton Court Palace.

**MOST LIKELY TO BE FOUND:** In Los Angeles, where his wife, Lady Frederick Windsor, works as a television actress. Freddie will continue to work for J.P. Morgan in their California offices.

# ZARA PHILLIPS, MBE

**BORN:** May 15, 1981

**ROYAL HERITAGE:** She is the eldest granddaughter of HM Queen Elizabeth II, and her first cousins are Princes William and Harry. Zara is thirteenth in line to the British throne.

**WHAT MAKES HER HOT:** Her rebellious nature (she once had a pierced tongue), athletic figure, and daring fashion sense. A world-class equestrian, Zara was selected to represent Britain at the 2008 Olympics until an injury forced her to withdraw.

**AWARDS:** MBE (Member of the British Empire) for services to equestrianism (2007), BBC Sports Personality of the Year (2006)

**QUOTE:** "The royal link doesn't make a difference in my sport. Everyone just gets on with it and works as hard as each other. That's what counts."

**EDUCATION:** Studied equine physiotherapy at Exeter University

**LOVE LIFE:** Dating hunky English Rugby star Mike Tindall since 2003. (Mike's season starts when hers finishes, but it means they can support each other while competing.) The couple announced their engagement in December 2010 and enjoyed a discreet wedding in Scotland on July 30, 2011.

**ENDORSEMENTS:** With her blond patrician looks, it's no surprise that Zara was asked to be the face of Rolex, Land Rover, and Musto. She is the first member of the royal family to accept commercial sponsorship, but views it as a financial necessity if she is to continue competing.

**ACTIVITIES (OTHER THAN RIDING):** Hockey, gymnastics, bungee jumping, hunting

**MOST LIKELY TO BE FOUND:** Cheering at Mike's rugby matches, practicing dressage with her horse, sipping cocktails at the Groucho Club, launching her own equestrian clothing line, planning her holiday home in Portugal.

**ZARA'S CHARITIES:**

◆ *The Catwalk Trust* Dedicated to finding a cure to spinal cord injury. Zara is an official patron. http://www.catwalk.org.nz/

◆ *The Mark Davies Injured Riders Fund* The only UK charity that helps those injured in horse-related accidents. Zara is an official patron. http://www.mdirf.co.uk/

# CHARLOTTE CASIRAGHI
# OF MONACO

**BORN:** August 3, 1986

**ROYAL HERITAGE:** Fourth in line to the Monegasque throne, her maternal grandmother was the glamorous screen star Grace Kelly; her brothers are the youthfully handsome Andrea and Pierre. As Monegasque titles only pass down through the male line, Charlotte was born without a royal title. In the hope that she might be able to lead a normal life, no additional titles were bestowed upon her.

**EDUCATION:** Degree in philosophy from the Sorbonne

**WHAT MAKES HER HOT:** Her sultry beauty, demure elegance, and irresistibly pouty lips. Not only does she resemble a young Angelina Jolie, Charlotte has a grace and maturity beyond her years. She is painfully stylish, quadro-lingual, and sophisticated beyond words. (According to British *Vogue*, she requested a Givenchy dress for her fifth birthday.) Gucci is currently designing her equestrian wardrobe.

**LOVE LIFE:** Linked to jet-setting Brazilian heartthrob and London gallery owner Alex Dellal.

**WORK:** Contributing editor for *Above Magazine*, founder of the eco-friendly fashion journal *Ever Manifesto*. (Charlotte's interest in the link between fashion and the environment grew after she befriended designer Stella McCartney.)

**LANGUAGES:** French, Italian, English, German

**ACTIVITIES:** Show jumping, promoting ethical fashion and sustainable living, skiing, snowboarding, swimming, Eastern philosophy, piano

**MOST LIKELY TO BE FOUND:** At international show-jumping competitions, gallery openings, St. Tropez, couture shows in Paris, the Monaco Grand Prix, sunning on the Italian island of Ponza, skiing in the Alps

**CHARLOTTE'S CHARITIES:**

◆ *Ever Manifesto* http://www.evermanifesto.com/

◆ *The Princess Grace Foundation* Supports pediatric medicine and humanitarian aid for handicapped children. http://www.fondation -psse-grace.mc/frameseteng.html

# HRH PRINCE CARL PHILIP OF SWEDEN

**BORN:** May 13, 1979

**ROYAL HERITAGE:** Second in line to the Swedish throne, behind his older sister Princess Victoria. His younger sister is the highly eligible Princess Madeleine.

**WHAT MAKES HIM HOT:** Smoldering Hollywood looks (he is a dead ringer for Orlando Bloom); impressive military service (he is trained as a combat boat commander); prize-winning design skills.

**EDUCATION:** Studied graphic design at the Rhode Island School of Design

**LOVE LIFE:** His long-term relationship with Emma Pernald ended in March 2009. He broke female hearts around the world when he began dating controversial glamour model Sofia Hellqvist in January 2010.

**ACTIVITIES:** Documentary photography, skiing, sailing, hunting, motor sports (he began competing in the Swedish Porsche Carrera Cup in 2008)

**PROJECTS:** The prince entered a prestigious competition (under a pseudonym) to develop a logo for the Martha's Vineyard Museum— and won! He's also designed his own line of contemporary sliver cutlery, which is for sale in Sweden. Carl Philip recently collaborated on a movie for National Geographic filmed on location in Borneo and has helped create a documentary to commemorate the three hundredth birthday of renowned Swedish botanist Carl von Linné.

**CARL PHILIP'S CHARITY:**

◆ *The World Childhood Foundation* Founded by his mother, HM Queen Silvia of Sweden, the charity helps street children, children living in institutions, young mothers, and sexually abused children. http://www.childhood.org/

# HRH PRINCESS EUGENIE OF YORK

**BORN:** March 23, 1990

**ROYAL HERITAGE:** Sixth in line to the British throne, her parents are Prince Andrew, the Duke of York, and Sarah, the Duchess of York (aka Fergie). Eugenie's grandmother is HM Queen Elizabeth II. Her first cousins are princes William and Harry.

**HOW TO PRONOUNCE HER NAME:** YOO-genny (*not* you-JAY-nee)

**WHAT MAKES HER HOT:** Her glossy hair, gamine features, sharp fashion sense, and free-spirited nature. (She infamously streaked to celebrate her school graduation.) She is also one of the brightest members of the Windsor family, with A-level exam results that broke all royal records.

**EDUCATION:** She is currently studying English and history of art at Newcastle University and has completed an internship at Christie's, the prestigious London auction house.

**ACTIVITIES:** Indie music, poetry, photography, tennis, skiing

**FAVORITE SNACK FOOD:** Hot dogs

**FAVORITE BOOK:** *Of Mice and Men*, by John Steinbeck

**FAVORITE TV SHOWS:** *Desperate Housewives*, *Lost*

**LOVE LIFE:** After breaking up with party-loving polo player Otto Brockway (nephew of Virgin tycoon Richard Branson), Eugenie has reportedly been dating London bartender Jack Brooksbank (four years her senior), whom she met in Verbier, an elite ski resort in the Swiss Alps.

**MOST LIKELY TO BE FOUND:** At house parties; private raves; smart London nightclubs like Public, Boujis, Mahiki, and the Cuckoo Club

**EUGENIE'S CHARITIES:**

- ◆ *Kids Company* Provides practical, emotional, and educational support to vulnerable inner city children and young people. http://www.kidsco.org.uk/
- ◆ *Children in Crisis* Improves the lives of children around the world affected by conflict, deprivation, and poverty. It was founded by Eugenie's mother, the Duchess of York. http://www.childrenincrisis.org/
- ◆ *Elephant Family* Works to save the Asian elephant from extinction and abuse. http://www.elephantfamily.org/

# PIERRE CASIRAGHI
# OF MONACO

**BORN:** September 5, 1987

**ROYAL HERITAGE:** Third in line to the Monegasque throne, this heart-throb is the younger brother of Charlotte and Andrea. His grandparents were the iconic Grace, Princess of Monaco, and Rainier III, Prince of Monaco.

**WHAT MAKES HIM HOT:** His piercing gray eyes, schoolboy charm, musical talent, and James Dean swagger

**EDUCATION:** Studied economics at Bocconi University in Milan. It is predicted that Pierre will go on to work for the companies of his late father Stefano Casiraghi, who passed away in 1990.

**LANGUAGES:** French, Italian, English, German

**ACTIVITIES:** Saxophone, soccer, martial arts, horseback riding, tennis, scuba diving

**LOVE LIFE:** Has been dating aristocratic beauty Beatrice Borromeo for over a year. Pierre met the Italian model/writer while studying in Milan, and they have been inseparable ever since. Both Pierre and Beatrice recently topped *Vanity Fair*'s coveted International Best-Dressed List in recognition of their youthful dynastic style.

**MOST LIKELY TO BE FOUND:** At bars and beaches of the Mediterranean, cruising the azure waters of St. Tropez, at the Monaco Grand Prix and the Tour de France

**PIERRE'S CHARITIES:**

◆ *AMADE* Founded in 1963 by HSH Princess Grace of Monaco to seek the promotion and protection of children's rights on an international level. Pierre plays in the annual charity soccer match. http://www.amade-mondiale.org/en

◆ *Asociación TATSA* Provides educational aid to students who were directly affected by the tsunami on December 26, 2004. http://www.tatsa.org/home.htm

◆ *The Princess Grace Foundation* Supports pediatric medicine and humanitarian aid for handicapped children. http://www.fondation-psse-grace.mc/frameseteng.html

# HRH CROWN PRINCE LEKA II OF ALBANIA

**BORN:** March 26, 1982, in Johannesburg. Although Leka was born in exile, the South African government declared his hospital room temporary Albanian territory to ensure that Leka was born on his own soil. Albania's dictatorship ended in the early nineties and the royal family was welcomed back.

**ROYAL HERITAGE:** Leka is the only child of King Leka I and Queen Susan.

**WHAT MAKES HIM HOT:** His earnest smile and dedication to his country (he works tirelessly toward stability in the Balkan region).

**EDUCATION:** Sandhurst Military Academy, during which time he was named "Best foreign student of the Academy"; BA in international relations and diplomacy from Royal University of Illyria.

**LANGUAGES:** Albanian, English, Italian

**LOVE LIFE:** In 2010, the prince married the beautiful brunette actress/singer Elia Zaharia in a Paris ceremony. (You can find several of her music videos on YouTube.)

**WORK:** Crown Prince Leka is the political advisor to the minister of interior.

**QUOTE:** "With the title of Prince comes responsibility and duty; to work for the needs of one's people and nation."

**ACTIVITIES:** Martial arts, chess, literature, skiing, golf

**FAVORITE MOVIE:** *The Matrix*

**FAVORITE TV SHOWS:** *Friends, Star Trek*

**LEKA'S CHARITY:**

◆ *SOS Orphans of Albania* Helps orphans and helps prevent families from abandoning their children. http://www.soschildrensvillages .ca/Where-we-help/Europe/Albania/Pages/default.aspx

PRECEDING PAGE:

Princess Florence Von Preussen (left) and shoe designer Alexandra Finlay

# PRINCESS FLORENCE VON PREUSSEN

**BORN:** July 28, 1983

**NICKNAME:** "Florrie"

**ROYAL HERITAGE:** Her parents are Prince Nicholas of Prussia and the Honorable Victoria Mancroft. She has one older sister, Princess Beatrice, and one younger sister, Princess Augusta—both of whom were beautiful debutantes. Her father is a direct descendant of Queen Victoria, making her Queen Victoria's great-great-great-great-granddaughter. She is also the great-great-granddaughter of the last German kaiser.

**WHAT MAKES HER HOT:** Her lissome beauty, passion for travel, natural rapport with children, and obvious talent for art and illustration.

**LOVE LIFE:** Dating financier Nat Rothschild (son of Lord Rothschild). Although he is twelve years her senior, many predict marriage is in the cards.

**WORK:** Formerly a teaching assistant at the exclusive Garden House School in Chelsea, Florrie now creates tailor-made illustrations for children's books and invitations.

# HIS IMPERIAL HIGHNESS PRINCE GEORG FRIEDRICH OF PRUSSIA

**BORN:** June 10, 1976, in Germany

**ROYAL HERITAGE:** His parents are Prince Louis-Ferdinand of Prussia and Countess Donata of Castell-Rüdenhausen; Prince Georg has been head of the Royal Family of Prussia (and therefore head of the Imperial House of Hohenzollern) since a court ruling in 1994, when he was just eighteen years old.

**WHAT MAKES HIM HOT:** His classic Ken Doll looks, wanderlust, spontaneity, and strong sense of duty

**EDUCATION:** Studied business economics at the Freiberg University of Mining and Technology; a six-month internship in Ecuador

**ACTIVITIES:** Prussian history, promoting German-American relations, technology, mountain biking, judo, tae kwon do, Spanish, traveling (he loves South America), hunting, shooting

**LOVE LIFE:** Married to aristocratic, German businesswoman Princess Sophie von Isenburg, whom he has known since childhood.

**GEORG'S CHARITY:**
◆ *The Princess Kira of Prussia Foundation* Founded by Georg's grandmother in 1952, the foundation provides free vacations for socially disadvantaged children at Hohenzollern Castle.

# MOST ELIGIBLE

*P*rince Harry is obviously the Holy Grail for lovelorn girls with royal taste, but it can't hurt to widen your net! Europe's monarchies are teeming with dozens upon dozens of hip twenty-somethings—many of them single and looking for love!

Do you suspect you were born for the regal life? Believe you were meant to live in palaces, attend charity galas, and wave to your adoring subjects on the arm of your royal spouse? Then fear not, future castle-dwellers! The following pages are filled with the most eligible young royals in the world. They're out there and they're worth catching.

These blue-blooded bachelors and bachelorettes are gorgeous, down-to-earth, and more than ready for romance. But in this increasingly media-driven age, they also face a great deal of pressure. Young royals must balance legions of unbridled admirers as well as unrestrained, often unfair, condemnation—all under the glare of the media spotlight. It's a tribute to their regal strength and character that these young people are able to carry it off with such grace and dignity.

Many suitors worry that their background may not be appropriate for a regal marriage, yet we must remember that it's no longer taboo for a royal to marry a commoner. In fact, now that William has married Kate, it's practically trendy to do so!

Keep in mind that if you carry yourself with confidence and poise, you have every right to rub shoulders with royalty. So be bold—do your research and study this section carefully. Discover the key to Prince Carl Philip's heart; find out what makes Princess Theodora melt; and ask yourself if you truly have what it takes to be a royal consort. Ready to live happily ever after? Then turn the page to meet the next generation of royal heartbreakers.

# HRH PRINCE HENRY (HARRY) OF WALES

**BORN:** September 15, 1984

**ROYAL HERITAGE:** Third in line to the British throne, he is the younger son of Prince Charles and the late Diana, Princess of Wales. His grandmother is HM Queen Elizabeth II.

**TRADEMARKS:** His laid-back magnetism, mischievous grin, passion for partying, daredevil nature and his mother's caring, empathic manner (just like Diana, Harry has a strong philanthropic spirit). Several years ago, he was entirely eclipsed by his dreamy older brother. But seemingly out of nowhere, Harry suddenly emerged as the hottest prince we've seen in decades! He may never inherit a kingdom, but that relieves him of responsibility and grants him the space to have a lot of fun.

**EDUCATION:** Eton College; gap year placement in Lesotho, Africa (where he worked with AIDS orphans as part of his *Forgotten Kingdom* documentary); Sandhurst Military Academy

**MILITARY SERVICE:** A lieutenant in the Household Cavalry, he is training to become a full-time Army Air Corps helicopter pilot.

**LOVE LIFE:** Dated blond Zimbabwean heiress Chelsy Davy on and off for over six years; they appear to have split permanently in 2010. This officially makes Harry the most eligible bachelor on the planet.

**ACTIVITIES:** Rugby (he is vice patron of England's Rugby Union), polo, skiing, surfing, wildlife, photography, off-road biking

**MOST LIKELY TO BE FOUND:** Watching rugby, playing polo, out and about in London (particularly Public, Mahiki, Boujis, and the Box), visiting his father at Highgrove, on a secret military mission

**QUOTE:** Harry often declares his determination to honor his mother's memory by embracing charity work that helps the disadvantaged: "I want to carry on the things she didn't quite finish," he says.[4]

**HOW TO WIN HIS HEART:** Get seriously involved with his charity work (and show him you are perfectly capable of clubbing till dawn).

**PRINCE HARRY'S CHARITIES:**

◆ *Sentebale* Founded by Prince Harry and Prince Seeiso of Lesotho in response to the plight of Lesotho's AIDS orphans and vulnerable children. The princes have a continuing role as active patrons. http://www.sentebale.org/

◆ *WellChild* Helps sick children and their families across the UK. Prince Harry is a patron and can often be seen chatting and joking with the children. http://www.wellchild.org.uk/

◆ *MapAction* Creates maps during natural disasters to highlight where medical attention is needed most. Prince Harry is a patron and is looking forward to training with them. http://www.mapaction.org/about.html

◆ *The Henry van Straubenzee Memorial Fund* Aims to lift Ugandan children out of poverty through education. (Henry van Straubenzee, a schoolmate and close friend of Prince Harry, was killed in a car crash in 2002.) Princes William and Harry are joint patrons. http://www.henryvanstraubenzeemf.org.uk/

◆ *Walking with the Wounded* Funds further education for seriously injured members of the armed forces, helping them rebuild their lives and return to work. Harry is a patron and recently joined a team of disabled servicemen as they trekked to the North Pole in aide of the charity. http://walkingwiththewounded.org.uk/

◆ *The Prince's Rainforests Project* Founded by Harry's father, the Prince of Wales, to discourage deforestation rates and show the vital link between rain forests and climate change. Princes William and Harry appeared alongside their father and an animated frog in a recent public awareness film. http://www.rainforestsos.org/

◆ *The Diana, Princess of Wales Memorial Fund* Established in September 1997 to continue his mother's humanitarian work throughout the world. http://www.theworkcontinues.org/

◆ *Dolen Cymru* Creates life-changing links between Wales and Lesotho in the fields of education, health, and civil society. Prince Harry is a patron. http://www.dolencymru.org/

# LADY GABRIELLA WINDSOR

**BORN:** April 23, 1981

**ROYAL HERITAGE:** Lord Freddie's younger sister, she is the only daughter of Prince and Princess Michael of Kent; her father is a first cousin of HM Queen Elizabeth II.

**TRADEMARKS:** Icy blond hair, perfect skin, demure composure, and sophisticated style. Gabriella is known for gracing social events in modest day suits, shift dresses, and evening gowns that flatter her statuesque figure.

**EDUCATION:** BA in comparative literature and Hispanic studies from Brown University; about to begin a PhD in anthropology at Oxford University.

**INTERNSHIPS:** *Vanity Fair*, Sotheby's

**WORK:** Freelance journalism. She's already written for *Country Life*, the *Evening Standard*, the *Spectator*, and the *Mail on Sunday*, using the byline Ella Windsor. She is also an official style ambassador for Ralph Lauren.

**LOVE LIFE:** Her high-profile relationship with handsome Indian journalist Aatish Taseer ended in 2006.

**ACTIVITIES:** Art, photography, parachute-jumping, tennis, horseback riding, yoga, healthy eating

**MOST LIKELY TO BE FOUND:** Shopping at London's flagship Whole Foods store on High Street Kensington

**HOW TO WIN HER HEART:** Make her a batch of fluffy, homemade waffles with hot maple syrup—her favorite American treat!

**GABRIELLA'S CHARITIES:**

- *The Naked Heart Foundation* Supports safe play environments for children in urban Russia. http://www.nakedheart.org/
- *Oxfam* A leading aid and development charity. www.oxfam.org.uk

# LADY KITTY SPENCER

**BORN:** December 28, 1990, in London, but has lived in Cape Town since 1995

**ROYAL HERITAGE:** Her father is Charles, the 9th Earl Spencer, and her mother is the former "It Girl" and model Victoria Lockwood. She is the niece of the late Diana, Princess of Wales. Princes William and Harry are her first cousins. Her ancestral home is Althorp, the three-hundred-acre estate in Northamptonshire. (Kitty is the modern equivalent of Keira Knightley's character in *The Duchess*).

**TRADEMARKS:** Sense of humor, good manners, strong-mindedness, her aunt's cover-girl looks, and the fact that she has zero interest in the spotlight.

**EDUCATION:** Reddam House in South Africa (she was a straight-A student); now studying politics and psychology at the University of Cape Town. She hopes one day to work for *Vanity Fair*.

**LOVE LIFE:** Her two-year relationship with professional surfer Jasper Eales ended in 2009; she is now linked to South African soccer player Larry Cohen.

**ACTIVITIES:** Reading about Jackie Kennedy and Marilyn Monroe, watching *Grey's Anatomy* on television, going on safari, fashion

**QUOTE:** "I'm a total geek and terrible at sport."[5]

**MOST LIKELY TO BE FOUND:** On the beach; relaxing in the Althorp library after dinner

**HOW TO WIN HER HEART:** Kitty is a jeans and T-shirt girl at heart, so don't try to impress her with anything glitzy. Instead, take her out for pizza on London's King's Road.

**KITTY'S CHARITIES:**

◆ *The Serpentine Gallery* A popular modern and contemporary art gallery in Hyde Park. Their summer party is one of the most sought-after events of the year. http://www.serpentinegallery.org/

◆ *The Diana, Princess of Wales Memorial Fund* Established in September 1997 to continue the princess's humanitarian work throughout the world. http://www.theworkcontinues.org/

# GRAND DUKE GUILLAUME
## OF LUXEMBOURG

**BORN:** November 11, 1981

**OFFICIAL TITLE:** HRH the Hereditary Grand Duke (not to be confused with his uncle, Prince Guillaume of Luxembourg)

**ROYAL HERITAGE:** Guillaume is the eldest child of Grand Duke Henri of Luxembourg and his wife Grand Duchess Maria Teresa. He became heir apparent to the crown of Luxembourg after his father's accession in 2000.

**EDUCATION:** Sandhurst Military Academy; political science at the University of Angers in France; BA in international relations from Brunel University

**LANGUAGES:** Spanish, French, German, English, Luxembourgish

**ACTIVITIES:** Sailing, skiing, tennis, swimming, piano, football, humanitarian work (Guillaume has traveled on charity missions to Nepal and Mexico).

**LOVE LIFE:** His relationship with Norwegian Pia Haraldsen (the King of Sweden's niece) ended in 2003.

**FUTURE WIFE:** Guillaume has revealed that his ideal royal bride would be elegant, humble, open-minded, and a keen sports and music enthusiast. He also hopes she would be interested in Luxembourg state issues and prepared to take on the responsibilities of a grand duchess.

**HOW TO WIN HIS HEART:** Surprise him with tickets to see the New York Giants—his all-time favorite team. (Later that evening, wow him with your political knowledge.)

**GUILLAUME'S CHARITIES:**

◆ *Kraizberg Foundation* A charitable institute for the disabled (Guillaume is board chairman).

◆ *Board of Economic Development of Luxembourg* (Guillaume is honorary chairman).

◆ *The Cycling Federation of Luxembourg* (Guillaume is a patron). http://www.fscl.lu

# HRH PRINCESS MADELEINE OF SWEDEN

**BORN:** June 10, 1982

**ROYAL HERITAGE:** Known as "Len" to her friends, she is the youngest of King Carl XVI Gustaf and Queen Silvia's three children. Born just eleven days before Prince William, pretty Princess Madeleine was once believed to be the perfect match for Britain's future king.

**TRADEMARKS:** Gorgeous golden skin, gorgeous golden locks, and her keen engagement in social issues

**EDUCATION:** BA in art, ethnology, and modern history from Stockholm University

**ACTIVITIES:** Horseback riding, skiing, art, dance, theater, long walks, nature, and gymnastics

**LOVE LIFE:** Princess Madeleine recently split from her fiancé, Jonas Bergström. They had been together for seven years and were expected to wed in late 2010.

**MOST LIKELY TO BE FOUND:** In the Big Apple; she has recently moved to New York City's Upper East Side.

**HOW TO WIN HER HEART:** With your loyalty. This young princess is not willing to have her heart broken a second time.

**QUOTE:** "At one point in my life I said to myself, I'm a princess—so what should I do? To just cut ribbons is not enough for me. I want to make a greater contribution. I believe that if everyone helped just a little, the world would be a better place. I know not everyone can afford to donate money, but you can do other things. You don't need to move mountains, but maybe pick up a piece of sand?"[6]

**MADELEINE'S CHARITIES:**

◆ *UNICEF* Fights for children's rights, their survival, development, and protection under the guidance of the Convention of the Rights of the Child. Madeleine interned for UNICEF's New York office. www.unicef.org

◆ *Min Stora Dag* Grants wishes to critically ill children who are suffering from life-threatening diseases. Princess Madeleine is a patron and regularly visits the children in the hospital. http://www.minstoradag.org/

◆ *World Childhood Foundation* Founded by Madeleine's mother, HM Queen Silvia of Sweden, the charity helps street children, children living in institutions, young mothers, and sexually abused children. http://www.childhood.org/

# HSH ALBERT, 12TH PRINCE OF THURN AND TAXIS

**BORN:** June 24, 1983, in Germany

**ROYAL HERITAGE:** His parents are Johannes, Prince of Thurn and Taxis, and Gloria, Princess of Thurn and Taxis. The name "Thurn" comes from the Italian word for *tower*, and "Taxis" from the word for *badger*.

**TRADEMARK:** Albert happens to be the world's third youngest billionaire (only Facebook moguls outrank him!). His family fortune stems from sixteenth-century postal services, breweries, and castle construction, as well as owning thirty thousand hectares of German woodland.

**EDUCATION:** Studied economics and theology at the University of Edinburgh

**ACTIVITIES:** Motor sports ("The Prince has gasoline in his blood," a tabloid once pronounced). Albert currently races for the German team Reiter Engineering.

**ECO-CAUSE:** Despite his love of burning fuel on the racetrack, the prince feels strongly about alternative energy. He is working to install solar panels with sixty-five-megawatt peak capacities on all his family lands in Bavaria.

**HOW TO WIN HIS HEART:** Surprise him with a romantic thrill ride in a vintage Lamborghini (but don't forget to offset your carbon footprint).

# HRH PRINCE FÉLIX OF LUXEMBOURG

**BORN:** June 3, 1984

**ROYAL HERITAGE:** Younger brother of Guillaume, Félix is the second son of Grand Duke Henri of Luxembourg and Grand Duchess Maria Teresa. Besides being Prince of Luxembourg, he is also Prince of Nassau.

**TRADEMARKS:** Techy brain, easygoing charm, debonair looks, and a passion for extreme sports

**EDUCATION:** Royal Military Academy of Sandhurst; a master's degree in bioethics from Regina Apostolorum Pontifical Athenaeum in Rome.

**LANGUAGES:** French, English, German

**ACTIVITIES:** Technology, basketball, billiards, tennis, soccer, golf, polo, skydiving, skiing, and other winter sports, like slalom snowboarding

**HOW TO WIN HIS HEART:** Whether it's freestyle skiing or tandem skydiving, Félix loves watching acrobatics. Surprise him with front row tickets to the latest Cirque du Soleil!

**FÉLIX'S CHARITIES:**

- *Luxembourg Federation of Basketball* Felix is honorary president. http://www.flbb.lu/
- *Cercle Para Luxembourg* (a skydiving organization) Felix is a patron. http://www.cerclepara.lu/

# HRH PRINCESS THEODORA
# OF GREECE AND DENMARK

**BORN:** June 9, 1983

**ROYAL HERITAGE:** Theodora is the youngest daughter and fourth child of King Constantine II of Greece and Queen Anne-Marie of Denmark. Three of her four grandparents are descendants of Queen Victoria. Her aunts include Queen Sofia of Spain and Queen Margrethe II of Denmark.

**TRADEMARKS:** Golden hair, dark green eyes, killer stage presence, and a tireless passion for the arts. She is also in the line of succession for both the Greek *and* British thrones.

**EDUCATION:** Northeastern University, Boston; Brown University, Rhode Island (where she received a BA in drama and performing arts—her stage name was Theodora Greece); Central Saint Martin's College of Art and Design, London

**ACTIVITIES:** Sailing, reading, theater, music, dance

**LOVE LIFE:** Has been seen stepping out with Hollywood actor Scott Elrod.

**MOST LIKELY TO BE FOUND:** Arts-related galas in Beverly Hills, Hollywood movie premieres, supporting the Los Angeles Dodgers, enjoying the annual Copa Del Rey regatta in Palma, Majorca

**HOW TO WIN HER HEART:** Surprise her with tickets to a quirky, off-Broadway play. Later that night, impress her by reciting one of Shakespeare's sonnets.

## THEODORA'S CHARITIES:

◆ *The Anna-Maria Foundation* Provides aid to people who have suffered due to natural disasters. Princess Theodora is a board member. http://www.greekroyalfamily.gr/index.cfm?get=foundation

◆ *The American Cancer Society* Supports cancer research, patient services, early detection, treatment, and education. Princess Theodora recently participated in the ACS Relay for Life. http://www.relayforlife.org/relay/

◆ *Rally for the Cure* A grassroots program that works to spread awareness about breast health and breast cancer. Princess Theodora recently attended a fund-raiser hosted by actress Eva Longoria. http://www.rftcpromotions.com

# HRH PRINCESS ALEXANDRA OF LUXEMBOURG

**BORN:** February 16, 1991

**ROYAL HERITAGE:** Younger sister of Guillaume and Félix. Through her father, Princess Alexandra is related to every currently reigning European monarch.

**TRADEMARKS:** Taking after Kate Middleton, Princess Alexandra is known for her glossy chestnut hair, elegant fashion sense, and quiet grace.

**EDUCATION:** Preparing for a degree in literature, history, and philosophy

**LANGUAGES:** Luxembourgish, French, English, German, Spanish

**ACTIVITIES:** Tennis, skiing, waterskiing

**HOW TO WIN HER HEART:** Princess Alexandra loves water sports, so charter a sailboat for a romantic sunset cruise along the Mediterranean coast.

**ALEXANDRA'S CHARITY:**

◆ *The International Paralympics* Promotes and creates sport opportunities for all persons with a disability, from beginner to elite levels. http://www.paralympic.org/

Crown Prince Alexander of Yugoslavia (center) and his wife, Princess Maria da Gloria of Orléans Bragança, with their sons (left to right) Hereditary Prince Peter, and fraternal twins Prince Philip and Prince Alexander.

# PRINCES PETER, ALEXANDER, AND PHILIP OF YUGOSLAVIA

**ROYAL HERITAGE:** Their parents are Crown Prince Alexander of Yugoslavia and Princess Maria da Gloria of Orléans Bragança.

**LANGUAGES:** English, Spanish, French, Serbian

**MOST LIKELY TO BE FOUND:** Skiing with the family in Zermatt, Switzerland

**THEIR CHARITY:**

◆ *The Crown Prince Alexander II Foundation for Education* Helps Serbian youth to attain quality education, successful careers, and personal fulfillment. http://pafond.rs/

## HRH HEREDITARY PRINCE PETER OF YUGOSLAVIA

**BORN:** February 5, 1980, in Chicago. As eldist he is first in line to the throne.

**EDUCATION:** London's Camberwell College of Arts; Rhode Island School of Design

**ACTIVITIES:** Scuba diving, snowboarding, surfing, music, painting, drawing, art, traveling, reading, graphic design

**HOW TO WIN HIS HEART:** Show him around your favorite art museum.

## HRH PRINCE PHILIP

**BORN:** January 15, 1982, in Fairfax, Virginia. HRH Prince Alexander is his fraternal twin brother. Philip was born first so he is second in line to the throne.

**EDUCATION:** BA from University College London; recently graduated from the esteemed Lausanne Hotel School in Switzerland. He currently resides in London.

**ACTIVITIES:** Painting, music, computer science, skateboarding, surfing, scuba diving, snowboarding

**HOW TO WIN HIS HEART:** Surprise him with a romantic dinner at Claridge's—London's historic and most sophisticated hotel. (His father was born there while in exile in 1945.)

## HRH PRINCE ALEXANDER

**BORN:** January 15, 1982, in Fairfax, Virginia. HRH Prince Philip is his fraternal twin brother. Alexander is third in line to the throne.

**EDUCATION:** BA in communications and media from the University of San Francisco; working toward an MA in fine art and art direction from American University. He resides in California.

**ACTIVITIES:** Art, photography, music, current affairs, surfing, snowboarding, scuba diving, museums, international cuisine, literature, tennis, basketball, soccer

**HOW TO WIN HIS HEART:** Prince Alexander is a culture buff with a passion for good food. Surprise him with tickets to the French cinema then cook up a romantic, candlelit dinner.

# PRINCESS ELISABETH OF THURN AND TAXIS

**BORN:** March 24, 1982, in Germany

**ROYAL HERITAGE:** Older sister of the eligible Prince Albert, her parents are Johannes, Prince of Thurn and Taxis, and Gloria, Princess of Thurn and Taxis. Her family's massive fortune is derived from their position as hereditary general postmasters of the Holy Roman Empire. She was a childhood friend of Lord Frederick Windsor.

**TRADEMARKS:** Long blond hair, regal cheekbones, and zeitgeist glamour

**EDUCATION:** BA from the American University of Paris

**WORK:** Princess Elisabeth is a regular contributor and blogger for *Finch's Quarterly Review*—a luxury lifestyle newspaper and website. Elisabeth has also written for *Quest* and *Monopol* magazines. She is currently working on a book about art collecting.

**ACTIVITIES:** Pilates, kite surfing, water-skiing, vintage fashion, art galleries, exhibitions

**MOST LIKELY TO BE FOUND:** At her summer home in Lake Starnberg, Germany, or her mother's house in Kenya; playing polo in Argentina; browsing Portobello Market, the Frieze Art Fair or the Saatchi Gallery in London.

**HOW TO WIN HER HEART:** Surprise with her a romantic afternoon at the Metropolitan Museum of Art, followed by cocktails at Manhattan's Boom Boom Room.

**ELISABETH'S CHARITY:**

◆ *The Order of Malta* Aims to help the sick, the needy, and the most disadvantaged in more than 120 countries. Elisabeth participates in the annual pilgrimage to Lourdes in aid of the elderly and disabled. http://www.orderofmalta.org/english

# HRH PRINCE PHILIPPOS OF GREECE AND DENMARK

**BORN:** April 26, 1986

**ROYAL HERITAGE:** The younger brother of Princess Theodora, Philippos is the youngest of King Constantine II of Greece and Queen Anne-Marie of Denmark's five children. Diana, Princess of Wales, was his godmother. Holding the title originally held by Queen Elizabeth II's husband, the Duke of Edinburgh, Philippos remains in the line of succession for both the Greek and British thrones.

**TRADEMARKS:** Tall, dark and handsome—Philippos is so charismatic that he was once considered for the UK television show *Celebrity Big Brother.*

**EDUCATION:** Hellenic College of London; United World College, New Mexico; and a degree in foreign relations from Georgetown University, Washington, DC.

**ACTIVITIES:** Computers, history, music, Rollerblading, swimming, soccer

**MOST LIKELY TO BE FOUND:** During happy hour at Manhattan's Hudson Terrace bar or out on the town in London.

**HOW TO WIN HIS HEART:** The prince is a big soccer fan, so surprise him with match tickets to see one of his favorite teams, Arsenal (England) or Panathinaikos (Greece).

**PHILIPPOS'S CHARITY:**
- *The Anna-Maria Foundation* Provides aid to people who have suffered due to natural disasters. Philippos is a board member. http://www.greekroyalfamily.gr/index.cfm?get=foundation

# LADY ELOISE ANSON

**BORN:** April 18, 1981, in London

**ROYAL HERITAGE:** Her late father was acclaimed royal photographer 5th Earl of Lichfield (aka Patrick Lichfield) and a cousin once removed of HM Queen Elizabeth II. Her mother is Lady Leonora Grosvenor. Lady Eloise is close friends with Prince William and Prince Harry.

**TRADEMARKS:** Her kooky personality, unique eye for fashion, and fantastic bone structure (she is said to be a muse for milliners—including Philip Treacy and the late Isabella Blow).

**EDUCATION:** Delamar Academy; Collingham College; studied prosthetics design at Ealing Studios.

**WORK:** Lady Eloise was a trainee in the special effects department at Leavesden Studios; her goal is to be part of the makeup crew for the next Harry Potter film.

**QUOTE:** "I think it's enormously important not to make a career on the back of my family name."[7]

**MOST LIKELY TO BE FOUND:** At Boujis, the Cuckoo Club, the Cock and Bottle, Le Quecum Bar.

**HOW TO WIN HER HEART:** Spend a romantic afternoon together in Battersea Park rose garden—one of her favorite spots in London.

**ELOISE'S CHARITY:**
- *The Stroke Association* Supports stroke survivors and their families in the UK. http://www.stroke.org.uk/

PRECEDING PAGE:

Princess Elena of Romania with her son Nicholas of Romania

# HRH PRINCE NICHOLAS OF ROMANIA

**BORN:** April 1, 1985, in Switzerland as Nicholas Medforth-Mills. He officially became Prince of Romania on his twenty-fifth birthday.

**ROYAL HERITAGE:** His parents are Dr. Robin Medforth-Mills and Princess Elena of Romania. Nicholas is currently in the line of succession to both the Romanian and British thrones. As Crown Princess Margareta of Romania is childless, it is likely that Nicholas will eventually succeed as the head of the Romanian Royal House and pretender to the throne. In a 2008 interview, Nicholas revealed that if the Romanian people ask him to become their king, he will not refuse.

**TRADEMARKS:** Charming smile, passion for adventure

**EDUCATION/WORK:** Shiplake College in Henley-on-Thames, Great Britain. He has since worked for World Challenge, an educational travel and adventure company. He now makes frequent trips to Romania and often accompanies his uncle, Prince Radu of Romania, on official engagements.

**ACTIVITIES:** Cars, boats, film, travel, rugby, hockey, soccer

**HOW TO WIN HIS HEART:** Show him your love for his country and your sense of fun, with tickets to a gala ball in aid of his favorite Romanian charity.

**NICHOLAS'S CHARITY:**
- *UNITER* Develops and promotes theater projects in Romania. http://www.uniter.ro/

# PRINCESS BEATRICE VON PREUSSEN OF PRUSSIA

**BORN:** February 10, 1981, in London

**ROYAL HERITAGE:** Her parents are Prince Nicholas of Prussia and the Honorable Victoria Mancroft; she is the eldest of their four children (her younger sisters Princesses Florence and Augusta are also highly eligible). Her father is a direct descendant of Queen Victoria, which makes Beatrice Queen Victoria's great-great-great-great-granddaughter.

**NICKNAME:** "Bee."

**TRADEMARKS:** Her stunning debut at the high society Crillion Ball in Paris, her passion for idiosyncratic design.

**EDUCATION:** Foundation course at Bournemouth Arts Institute; later specialized in plastics, ceramics, and metalwork at Brighton University.

**WORK:** Princess Beatrice was consulted by children's author Susanna Davidson for the royal content contained in *The Princess Handbook* (Usborne Publishing, 2006), which provides "expert advice from a real princess." In 2007, Beatrice cofounded The Studio Shop in Brighton, UK, where she exhibits and sells her own artwork as well as pieces from other local artists. The Studio Shop also serves as a venue for exhibitions, installations, and small performances.

**MOST LIKELY TO BE FOUND:** Shopping for Vivienne Westwood frocks, relaxing at her family home in Somerset.

**HOW TO WIN HER HEART:** Make sure you know your way around a dance floor!

# HRH PRINCE AMEDEO
# OF BELGIUM

**BORN:** February 21, 1986

**OTHER TITLES:** Prince Imperial and Archduke of Austria-Este, Prince Royal of Hungary and Bohemia.

**ROYAL HERITAGE:** His parents are Lorenz, Archduke of Austria-Este, and Princess Astrid of Belgium.

**TRADEMARK:** Heart-stopping combination of brains and brawn.

**EDUCATION:** Royal Military Academy in Brussels; London School of Economics (LSE).

**WORK:** Reportedly working at Deloitte's global headquarters in New York City.

**ACTIVITIES:** Travel, Spanish, sports. Prince Amedeo played rugby for LSE and ran the New York Marathon alongside his father in 2007.

**HOW TO WIN HIS HEART:** Go jogging together in Central Park.

**AMEDEO'S CHARITY:**

◆ *The Queen Elisabeth Medical Foundation* Promotes and supports neuroscience research. Amedeo's mother, HRH Princess Astrid, is honorary president of the board of directors. http://www.fmre -gske.be/pages/en/interest.html

# CERTAIN THE ROYAL LIFE IS FOR YOU?

Study the regal prerequisites on this royal checklist and find out if you really have what it takes to wear a crown.

- ❏ *Education.* A high school diploma with a stint at Swiss finishing school is no longer sufficient. These days, reigning royals must have at least one college degree, if not several. Fluency in multiple languages is also a plus.

- ❏ *Career.* Princess Diana showed us that we can't always count on the prince. Forge a career in what you love—be it journalism, advertising or banking—and rest assured that the skills you learn in the business world (leadership, diplomacy, hard work) will serve you well in your future royal role.

- ❏ *Self-belief.* Ignore your critics. If you know in your heart that you are worthy of a prince or princess, don't let anyone tell you otherwise.

- ❏ *Style.* Forget fashion trends and stick with the classics. Perfect the art of "conservative chic" and learn to love cashmere and tweed.

- ❏ *Manners.* A true princess behaves like a princess no matter what the circumstances. Traditional etiquette is not about being superior to others, but about making those around you feel comfortable. So study up on continental dining, make sure you know how to curtsey, and always (always) write thank-you notes.

❑ *True Love.* Palaces and jewels can come and go, and many ancient royal families are not nearly as wealthy as they seem. Make sure that you're with your prince or princess for love and not simply for status.

❑ *Discretion.* No matter how much you want to tell your friends what goes on behind palace walls; no matter how much your royal in-laws drive you crazy—you must keep it to yourself. No gossip. No tell-all interviews. Just dignified silence.

❑ *Patience.* Can you shake thousands of hands a day and keep smiling even if you have a headache? Can you sit through endless hours of presentations, speeches, parades, and processions, month after month, year after year, without yawning even once?

❑ *Service.* A prince or princess must look beyond themselves in every situation, place their duty to the realm before all else, and always use their privileged position toward the greater good.

❑ *Compassion.* Wherever royals go, the press is sure to follow. Make sure you have the courage to draw the world's attention away from yourself and onto those that need it most.

❑ *Self-reliance.* Remember that happily-ever-after is a state of mind you have to create—every day, every moment—for yourself.

# MORE TITLED
# TALENT

F rom English polo fields to London nightclubs, from the snowy ski runs of the Swiss Alps to the dusty plains of Africa, our young royals can be found out and about with other gifted and glamorous young aristocrats. We've handpicked the best and brightest of the bunch.

# HRH PRINCE ALEXANDER OF SAXE-COBURG AND GOTHA

**WHO IS HE?** A royal with superb pedigree and a heartbreaking smile

**BORN:** May 4, 1977, in Coburg, Germany

**FULL NAME:** Alexander Philipp

**FULL TITLE:** His Royal Highness Prince of Saxe-Coburg and Gotha, Duke of Saxony

**ROYAL HERITAGE:** His father is Prince Andreas of Saxe-Coburg and Gotha, a great-grandson of Queen Victoria's youngest son, Prince Leopold. Alexander has one older brother, Hereditary Prince Hubertus, and one older sister, Princess Stephanie.

# HSH PRINCE CARLOS VON HOHENZOLLERN

**WHO IS HE?** A high-achieving creative type with a passion for the environment

**BORN:** December 4, 1978, in Munich, Germany

**FULL NAME:** Carlos Patrick Godehard

**FULL TITLE:** His Serene Highness Prince von Hohenzollern

**ROYAL HERITAGE:** His parents are Prince von Hohenzollern and Heide Hansen. Carlos has one younger sister, Princess Anna.

**WORK:** Educated in London, Prince Carlos worked as an account director for Saatchi and Saatchi before taking up the role of managing director at the BBDO advertising network. He now leads a $500 million green fund for Florida-based biofuel company InfoSpi and in 2010 was appointed to their board of directors.

**CHARITY:**

◆ *The Motrice Foundation* Supports cerebral palsy research. http://eng
.lafondationmotrice.org

PRECEDING PAGE:

Prince Francois (left) and his cousin Foulques D'Orléans (right)

# PRINCE FOULQUES OF ORLÉANS

**WHO IS HE?** An ancient French prince with a handsome head of floppy hair

**BORN:** July 9, 1974, in Paris

**FULL NAME:** Foulques Thibaut Robert Jacques Géraud Jean Marie

**FULL TITLE:** Prince of Orléans, Petit-fils of France, Comte of Êu, Duke of Aumâle

**ROYAL HERITAGE:** His parents are Prince Jacques of Orléans and Gersende de Sabran Pontevès. He has an older brother, Charles-Louis, and an older sister, Diane. The prince's paternal grandfather was the late Henri, Count of Paris, and is generally recognized as the rightful claimant to the French throne with the title Henri VI.

# HRH PRINCESS CAROLINA OF BOURBON-PARMA

**WHO IS SHE?** A dashing Dutch blonde with a humanitarian heart

**BORN:** June 23, 1974, in the Netherlands

**FULL NAME:** Maria-Carolina Christina

**FULL TITLE:** Her Royal Highness Princess of Bourbon-Parma, Marchioness of Sala, Duchess of Guernica

**ROYAL HERITAGE:** Carolina is the fourth and youngest child of Princess Irene of the Netherlands and Carlos Hugo, Duke of Parma. She is the niece of Queen Beatrice of the Netherlands.

**EDUCATION:** She studied political science and international relations at the University of Amsterdam and at Harvard University.

**WORK:** During her work for the United Nations, Princess Carolina has been based in New York, Geneva, Gaza, and Indonesia.

# PRINCESS ALIX OF LIGNE

**WHO IS SHE?** A gorgeous Belgian debutante

**BORN:** July 3, 1984, in Brussels

**FULL NAME:** Alix Marie Isabelle

**FULL TITLE:** Her Highness Princess Alix of Ligne

**ROYAL HERITAGE:** Her parents are Michel, 14th Prince of Ligne, and Princess Eleonora de Orléans e Bragança; she has one younger brother, Henri.

**FAMILY:** Dating back to the eleventh century, the House of Ligne is one of oldest noble families in Belgium. Her royal background allowed Princess Alix to debut at the prestigious Crillon Ball in Paris in 2009.

# PRINCESS AUGUSTA
# VON PREUSSEN

**WHO IS SHE?** The youngest Von Preussen princess

**BORN:** December 15, 1986, in London

**FULL NAME:** Augusta Lily

**ROYAL HERITAGE:** Her parents are Prince Nicholas of Prussia and the Honorable Victoria Mancroft. She is the youngest sister of the afore-mentioned Princesses Beatrice and Florence. Her father is a direct descendant of Queen Victoria, making her Queen Victoria's great-great-great-great-granddaughter.

**MOST LIKELY TO BE FOUND:** At elite fashion parties in London.

# PRINCESS FELIPA OF BAVARIA

**WHO IS SHE?** A German princess devoted to disabled children

**BORN:** February 1, 1981, in Germany

**FULL NAME:** Maria Felipa Karin Marion Gabriele

**FULL TITLE:** Her Royal Highness Princess of Bavaria

**ROYAL HERITAGE:** Her parents are Prince Leopold of Bavaria (the former race car driver and godfather to Prince Carl Philip of Sweden) and Princess Ursula; Felipa has three siblings.

**CHARITY:**

◆ *The Special Olympics* The world's largest sports organization for children and adults with disabilities. http://www.specialolympics.org

# PRINCESS MARIA ANUNCIATA AND PRINCESS MARIE ASTRID OF LIECHTENSTEIN

**WHO ARE THEY?** Stunning sisters descended from the royal houses of both Luxembourg and Liechtenstein

**ROYAL HERITAGE:** Their parents are Nikolaus, Prince of Liechtenstein, and Margaretha, Princess of Luxembourg. They have two brothers, Leopold and Josef.

**ADDRESS THEM AS:** Your Serene Highness

**FULL NAME:** Princess Maria Anunciata Astrid Joséphine Veronica of Liechtenstein

**BORN:** May 12, 1985, in Brussels

**STUDIED:** History of art in London

**FULL NAME:** Princess Marie Astrid Nora Margarita Veronica of Liechtenstein

**BORN:** June 26, 1987, in Brussels

**STUDIED:** Literature and languages in London. She also spent time in Argentina to practice her Spanish.

# PRINCESS XENIA OF SAXONY

**WHO IS SHE?** "The Frog Princess"

**BORN:** August 20, 1986, in Düsseldorf, Germany

**FULL NAME:** Xenia "Xeni" Florence Gabriela Sophie Iris

**ROYAL HERITAGE:** Her mother is Princess Iris von Sachsen; her grandfather is Prince Georg Timo von Sachsen.

**MOST LIKELY TO BE FOUND:** In the BBC dating documentary *Undercover Princesses* and working as an official ambassador for the "Year of the Frog" campaign to promote a cleaner environment for amphibians.

**CHARITY:**

◆ *Amphibian Ark* Aims to ensure the global survival of amphibians, focusing on those that cannot currently be safeguarded by nature. http://www.amphibianark.com

# PRINCE LUDWIG ZU HOHENLOHE-LANGENBURG

**WHO IS HE?** A prince with a gift for languages and love of the outdoors

**BORN:** April 12, 1976, in Germany

**FULL NAME:** Ludwig Ferdinand Ruprecht

**FULL TITLE:** His Serene Highness Prince zu Hohenlohe-Langenburg

**ROYAL HERITAGE:** His parents are Albrecht Prince zu Hohenlohe-Langenburg and Maria Fischer.

**LANGUAGES:** German, English, Latin, and Greek

**ACTIVITIES:** Computers, sailing, mountain biking

# PRINCE CHRISTIAN OF HANOVER

**WHO IS HE?** A prince with schoolboy charm and family links to the Monegasque throne

**BORN:** June 1, 1985, in Germany

**FULL NAME:** Christian Heinrich Clemens Paul Frank Peter Welf Ernst-Wilhelm Friedrich Franz

**FULL TITLE:** His Royal Highness Prince of Hanover

**ROYAL HERITAGE:** His father is Ernst August V, Prince of Hanover, his stepmother is Princess Caroline of Monaco, and his stepsiblings are the aforementioned Charlotte, Andrea, and Pierre of Monaco. Christian is also in the line of succession to the British throne.

# COUNT GIAN LUCA PASSI DE PREPOSULO

**WHO IS HE?** A well-dressed nobleman with a heart of gold

**BORN:** November 10, 1982, in Italy

**ROYAL HERITAGE:** His aristocratic family hails from Bergamo and dates back to the end of the first millennium (A.D. 973).

**PASSIONS:** Armani suits and Bono's Red Campaign

**QUOTE:** "It's not the title that's important—you have to be a count inside yourself."[8]

# HRH PRINCE ERNST AUGUST OF HANOVER

**WHO IS HE?** A prince with dark tousled hair and plenty of regal siblings

**BORN:** July 19, 1983, in Germany

**FULL TITLE:** HRH Ernst August, Prince of Hanover, Prince of Great Britain and Ireland, Duke of Brunswisk and Luneburg

**ROYAL HERITAGE:** His father is Ernst August V, Prince of Hanover (yes—it can get confusing!); his younger brother is the aforementioned Prince Christian; his stepmother is Princess Caroline of Monaco; Andrea, Charlotte, and Pierre are stepsiblings. He is also in the line of succession to the British throne.

PRECEDING PAGE:

Wedding of Prince Christian zu Füerstenberg and Jeanette Griesel

# HSH HEREDITARY PRINCE CHRISTIAN ZU FÜRSTENBERG

**WHO IS HE?** An exceedingly handsome prince who loves fast horses

**BORN:** November 22, 1977, in Germany

**ROYAL HERITAGE:** His parents are Prince Heinrich zu Fürstenberg and Princess zu Windisch. Prince Christian is the sole heir to the house of Fürstenberg, one of Germany's oldest and most significant noble families, which dates back to 1070.

**LANGUAGES:** German, English, French, Spanish, Italian

**ACTIVITIES:** President of the German Racing Association of Arabian Horses

**LOVE LIFE:** Married to Bavarian businesswoman Jeanette Griesel

**CHARITY:**

◆ *Order of Malta* Aims to help the sick, the needy, and the most disadvantaged in more than 120 countries. http://www.orderofmalta.org/english

# HIS IMPERIAL HIGHNESS
# THE GRAND DUKE
# GEORGE OF RUSSIA

**WHO IS HE?** A brainy royal hugely dedicated to the Russian Dynasty

**BORN:** March 13, 1981, in Madrid

**ROYAL HERITAGE:** He is the son of Prince Franz Wilhelm of Prussia and Grand Duchess Maria Vladimirovna of Russia; his godfather is King Constantine II of Greece. George is also in the line of succession to the British throne.

**EDUCATION:** Oxford University

**LANGUAGES:** English, French, Spanish

# CINDERELLA STORIES

*H*ave you always dreamed of marrying a handsome prince in a faraway kingdom? These women have done just that! Proving to the world that fairy tales really can come true, Kate Middleton has joined the tiara-wearing ranks of Princess Letizia of Spain, Princess Mette-Marit of Norway, Princess Mary of Denmark, and Princess Masako of Japan—all of whom are causing a frenzy of princess mania to sweep across the globe.

Think you have to come from aristocratic stock to be a princess? Think again. None of these glamorous consorts have a smidgen of blue blood running through their veins. Traditionalists are probably outraged, but at some point princesshood officially became an equal opportunity industry.

Just like the new Princess Catherine, the gorgeous Mary, Letizia, Masako, and Mette-Marit all hail from ordinary, hardworking backgrounds. And though none were born into royalty, each more than looks the part of a modern-day princess—moving with graceful ease from jeans to jewels. But not only are these women impeccably stylish, they also have brains and rather intimidating résumés that boast far more than the usual string of curtseys and dinner parties. Most importantly, now that they are firmly ensconced in their royal roles, all four princesses have immersed themselves in charity work in a way that would make the late Princess of Wales very, very proud.

Read on to see how each young woman won the heart of her prince, how their royal romance blossomed, and how each regal couple continue to electrify the adoring public. And don't forget, if it can happen to them, it can happen to you. . . .

# CROWN PRINCE FELIPE OF SPAIN AND LETIZIA, PRINCESS OF ASTURIAS

**HIM:** Born January 30, 1968, Felipe is the third child and only son of King Juan Carlos and Queen Sofía of Spain. After stints in all three branches of the armed forces, the prince graduated from the Autonomous University of Madrid before earning his master's degree in Foreign Service from Georgetown University (where he shared a student room with his cousin, Crown Prince Pavlos of Greece).

Gregarious and outgoing, Felipe speaks Spanish, Catalan, French, English, and some Greek. Tall (a towering six feet, three inches!), dark, and handsome, the prince is an avid skier and keen sailor (he sailed for Spain during the 1992 Barcelona Olympics). In addition to his royal charm and heartthrob looks, Prince Felipe is also said to have inherited his father's strong diplomacy and his mother's humanitarian spirit.

**HER:** Born September 15, 1972, Letizia comes from a very normal family—her father worked as a journalist and her mother as a hospital nurse. She graduated from Complutense University of Madrid, before earning her master's degree from the Institute for Studies in Audiovisual Journalism and eventually became an award-winning television reporter—working for CNN, ABC, and Bloomberg, among others. Prior to meeting her prince, Letizia reported from some of the world's most hostile environments. She covered the 2000 U.S. presidential election, broadcast live from Ground Zero after the September 11, 2001, attacks, and reported from the front lines of the Iraq War. Letizia fell in love with the handsome Prince Felipe in 2002, when she was sent to northern Spain to cover the ecological disaster caused by a sinking oil tanker.

**THEIR REGAL ROMANCE:** Prince Felipe always insisted that when he ultimately chose his princess, it would be "a relationship based on love, respect and kindness." He seems to have met his match in the beautiful, thoroughly modern Letizia, who is independent, cultured, and exceedingly accomplished. Although the couple had met once before at a dinner party, during their second meeting they couldn't keep their eyes off each other and began secretly dating almost immediately. The public was none the wiser until their official engagement was announced. Although Letizia was a divorcée (something that would not have been tolerated for a royal bride in the past), the public were delighted that their country would have a Spanish queen for the first time since 1879. Letizia quickly overcame any controversy and was openly embraced by the Spanish people, who happily view her as the figurehead of a new era and a "queen for the twenty-first century." Felipe and Letizia married in Madrid on the morning of May 22, 2004.

**HEIRS AND SPARES:** Princess Leonor (born October 31, 2005) and Princess Sofia (born April 29, 2007)

**PHILANTHROPY OF THE PRINCE AND PRINCESS:**

◆ *The Codespa Foundation* Helps poor communities with health, educational, and vocational training programs in Asia, Africa, and the Americas. Founded in 1985 and based in Spain, Crown Prince Felipe is the honorary president. http://www.codespa.org/

◆ *The Príncipe de Asturias Foundation* Promotes scientific, cultural, and humanistic values. Each year the foundation bestows the prestigious Prince of Asturias Awards, rewarding technical and social achievements. Crown Prince Felipe is the honorary president. http://www.fpa.es/en/

# CROWN PRINCE HAAKON AND CROWN PRINCESS METTE-MARIT OF NORWAY

**HIM:** Born July 20, 1973, Prince Haakon's parents are King Harald V and Queen Sonja. He was educated at the University of California at Berkeley, the University of Oslo, and the London School of Economics, where he studied International Politics, Law, and Social Science. Handsome and athletically built, Haakon loves to sail, ski, surf, and cycle. He is also an avid patron of the arts with a deep passion for theater, music, and literature. Haakon became Crown Prince of Norway on the death of his grandfather in 1991. When he married Mette-Marit in 2001, Crown Prince Frederik of Denmark served as his best man.

**HER:** Born August 19, 1973, Mette-Marit has no royal heritage—her father was a journalist and her mother worked in a bank. Like Haakon, she adores anything to do with sailing. In her wild youth, this Gwyneth Paltrow look-alike frequented raves and enjoyed dancing to house music. ("I certainly didn't have any ball gowns before I met Haakon!" she says.[9]) This party girl already had a three-year-old son (out of wedlock) when she met the crown prince through mutual friends, but despite the initial scrutiny, Norwegians were soon bowled over by her Nordic beauty, graceful intelligence, and unassuming demeanor.

**THEIR REGAL ROMANCE:** A single-mother princess with a child fathered by a man who has been linked to drug dealing? How could it possibly be? Well, when Crown Prince Haakon set eyes on this elegant Hitchcock blonde at a rock concert, he didn't think twice about her less-than-perfect past. Totally smitten, the prince shocked the world by welcoming Mette-Marit and her son Marius into his home, and within months he proposed to her.

At first there was public backlash to such an unconventional royal match (and the fact that the couple were "living in sin"), but Norway's king and queen remained supportive, and Mette-Marit won praise for her courage when she made a public statement expressing regret for her past. Haakon married Mette-Marit on August 25, 2001, at Oslo Cathedral, and the title of crown princess was bestowed upon her. She is now fervently adored by her subjects.

**HEIRS AND SPARES:** Princess Ingrid (born January 21, 2004) and Prince Sverre (born December 3, 2005). Marius Borg Høiby (born January 13, 1997) is not in the line of succession, but is very much part of the Norwegian royal family.

### PHILANTHROPY OF THE PRINCE AND PRINCESS:
◆ *The Crown Prince and Crown Princess' Humanitarian Fund* enables Haakon and Mette-Marit to focus efforts on humanitarian causes of special interest to them. In Norway, grants are allocated to projects aimed at improving conditions for children and young people. In countries abroad, the fund targets projects related to health and education. http://www.kongehuset.no/c28624/liste/vis.html?strukt _tid=28624

### HRH CROWN PRINCE HAAKON IS ALSO THE PATRON OF:
◆ 4H Norge—Norwegian 4H Organisation
◆ The Christian Radich Sail Training Foundation
◆ The Ibsen Stage Festival
◆ Nordland Music Festival
◆ The Northern Light Festival
◆ The Norwegian Association Against Substance Abuse
◆ The Norwegian Asthma and Allergy Association
◆ The Norwegian Band Federation
◆ The Norwegian Festival of International Literature
◆ The Norwegian International Film Festival

- The Norwegian Lifesaving Society
- Stavanger Symphony Orchestra
- Ultima Oslo Contemporary Music Festival

**HRH CROWN PRINCESS METTE-MARIT IS ALSO PATRON OF:**

- Amandus Film Festival
- FOKUS—Forum for Women and Development
- Kristians and International Children's Film Festival
- Risør Festival of Chamber Music
- The Norwegian Design Council
- The Norwegian Guide and Scout Association
- The Norwegian Red Cross
- The Norwegian Council for Mental Health
- Oslo International Church Music Festival

# CROWN PRINCE FREDERIK AND CROWN PRINCESS MARY OF DENMARK

**HIM:** Born May 26, 1968, Frederik is the elder son of Queen Margrethe II and Prince Henrik of Denmark and heir to the Danish throne (Europe's oldest monarchy). He studied political science at Harvard University, worked with the Danish UN mission in New York and later the Danish embassy in Paris, before eventually earning his MSc from the University of Aarhus. The dashing prince has also completed training with all three military services, most notably with the elite Royal Frogmen Corps (the naval Special Forces). Frederik once said, "I want to be a good ambassador for my country. But I will not shut myself away in a castle. I will be myself. I will be a human being."[10] Easygoing, fun-loving, and incredibly popular with the Danish people, Prince Frederik has a well-known penchant for adventure (including polar dog sledding and jungle treks) and has run marathons in Copenhagen, New York, and Paris.

**HER:** Born February 5, 1972, Mary is the youngest of four children. Incredibly down-to-earth, she was raised by her Scottish parents in Australia, where her father worked as a mathematics professor and her mother as a secretary. After graduating from university, the raven-haired beauty moved swiftly into a dazzling advertising career, including stints with high-flying companies like Young & Rubicam and Microsoft. Simple and chic, Mary is known for her classic-yet-modern taste, causing many observers to draw comparisons to Jackie Kennedy and Audrey Hepburn. Mary once said of her girlhood dreams, "I don't recall ever wishing to become a princess. I wanted to be a veterinarian!" But her ordinary life was forever changed one night in a pub, when she met a young man who introduced himself as "Fred."

**THEIR REGAL ROMANCE:** Crown Prince Frederik of Denmark met Mary at the Slip Inn during the 2000 Sydney Olympics. Never mind that she was a commoner; Frederik knew instantly that he had met the princess of his dreams. Not only was Mary undeniably beautiful, she was natural, relaxed, stylish, and sensible. She also loved horseback riding and all outdoor sports, just as he did. The prince was smitten. The starry-eyed couple embarked upon a discreet long-distance relationship until their engagement was officially announced in October 2003. They married on May 14, 2004, in Copenhagen Cathedral.

**HEIRS AND SPARES:** Prince Christian (born October 15, 2005) and Princess Isabella (born April 21, 2007). On January 8, 2011, Denmark rejoiced when Mary gave birth to twins, Prince Vincent and Princess Josephine.

**PHILANTHROPY OF THE PRINCE AND PRINCESS:**

- *The Mary Foundation* aims to advance the understanding of cultural diversity, prevent social isolation, and encourage tolerance, with a focus on bullying, well-being, and domestic violence. It was established in 2007 by HRH Crown Princess Mary of Denmark, who is the acting chairman. http://www.maryfonden.dk/Home.aspx

**HRH THE CROWN PRINCESS IS ALSO THE PATRON OF THE FOLLOWING:**

- The Children's Choir of the Royal Danish Academy of Music
- The Danish Arts and Crafts Association
- The Danish Cultural Institute
- Copenhagen International Fashion Fair
- Designers Nest
- The Danish Refugee Council (DRC)
- The Danish Youth Association of Science
- Research Day
- Children's Aid Foundation
- Danish Association for Mental Health

- LOKK (a nationwide organization of shelters for battered women)
- Maternity Worldwide
- Mothers Help
- Rare Disorders Denmark
- The Alannah & Madeline Foundation
- The Christmas Seal Foundation
- The Danish Brain Injury Association
- The Danish Heart Association
- The Danish Kidney Association
- The Danish Mental Health Fund
- The Danish Stroke Association
- World Health Organization
- The Danish Golf Union
- The Danish Swimming Federation

**HRH THE CROWN PRINCE IS THE PATRON OF THE FOLLOWING ORGANIZATIONS:**
- Aarhus University Male Choir
- The Anders Lassen Foundation
- The Association of Fine Arts
- The Associations of the Guard Hussars
- The Blood Donors in Denmark
- The Commission for Scientific Research in Greenland
- Copenhagen International Furniture Fair
- The Danish Association of the Hard of Hearing
- Danish Deaf Association
- Danish Design Center
- The Danish Dyslexia Organisation
- The Danish Military Sports Association
- The Danish National Committee of United World Colleges
- The Danish Naval Officers' Club
- The Danish Pleasure Crafts Safety Board
- Danish Railway Museum in Odense
- The Danish Tennis Association

- The Foreign Policy Society
- The Georg Jensen Prize
- The Greenlandic Society
- The Greenlandic Christmas-Seal Foundation
- The Naval-Lieutenant-Society
- Odense International Film Festival
- Plant a Tree
- Royal Academy of Music, Aarhus
- Royal Awards for Sustainability
- Save the Children Fund
- The Soldiers' Grant

# THEIR IMPERIAL HIGHNESSES CROWN PRINCE NARUHITO AND CROWN PRINCESS MASAKO

**HIM:** Born February 23, 1960, Prince Naruhito (known as Prince Hiro) is the oldest son of Emperor Akihito and heir to the Chrysanthemum Throne of Japan—the world's oldest hereditary monarchy. A graduate of History and Humanities from Gakushuin University, the prince has also studied at Oxford University in the UK and published a memoir about the experience entitled *The Thames and I*. His hobbies include jogging, hiking, mountaineering, and playing the viola. The prince remains a robust advocate for water conservation and other green causes—frequently acting as a keynote speaker on the subject. It has been said that the prince was completely smitten with the beautiful and intelligent Masako the first time he saw her.

**HER:** Born December 9, 1963, Masako was hardly a ditzy aristocrat. The eldest daughter of Mr. Hisashi Owada (a professor and diplomat), the teenage Masako attended an American high school outside of Boston, where she had a 4.0 GPA and became president of the National Honor Society. She continued her education at Harvard (magna cum laude) and Oxford, never suspecting that one day she would be a princess. Masako speaks no fewer than five languages (English, French, German, Russian, and Japanese) and passed Japan's Foreign Ministry entrance exam in record time. She is smart, charming, thoroughly modern, and seems to get along with everyone she meets. "She's always had the qualities of an empress," a friend once said.

**THEIR REGAL ROMANCE:** Crown Prince Naruhito ardently pursued and eventually proposed to the then twenty-nine-year-old Masako, who was working as a professional diplomat in the Japanese Foreign Ministry. But Masako wasn't interested in giving up her career, so she gently declined the prince's proposal—twice! Still, the prince persevered until Masako accepted. ("You might have fears and worries about joining the imperial household," he reportedly said to her, "but I will protect you for my entire life.") On June 9, 1993, the couple were married in a picture-perfect traditional Japanese wedding ceremony. Masako became the second commoner ever to enter the Japanese imperial household, but despite this lack of noble breeding, she is next in line to become Empress of Japan.

**HEIR:** Her Imperial Highness Princess Aiko (born December 1, 2001); her official title is *Toshi no Miya*, or Princess Toshi. However, females cannot inherit the Chrysanthemum Throne, so unless changes are made to the male-only law of imperial succession, Aiko will never be empress of Japan; rather the throne will pass to her cousin Prince Hisahito of Akishino.

**PHILANTHROPY OF THE PRINCE AND PRINCESS:**
- *The Japanese Red Cross Society* Conducts relief activities when major disasters strike. The crown prince and princess are honorary vice presidents. http://www.jrc.or.jp/english/index.html
- *The World Water Forum* Seeks to identify, promote, and develop concrete solutions for water. The crown prince has served as honorary president. http://www.worldwaterforum.org/
- *The Asia-Pacific Water Summit* Generates awareness to the significance of water issues and challenges. The crown prince lectured at the opening ceremony. http://www.adb.org/Water/apwf/apws/default.asp

# RECENT ROYAL BRIDES

*T*here can be no doubt that the world loves a royal wedding.

Royal nuptials are a fascinating mix of ancient tradition and modern-day opulence resulting in a heady concoction of romance, ritual, and old-fashioned fairy tale magic. If televised, they are watched by millions (sometimes billons); if photos are published, magazines sell out in a flash. There is just something about a royal wedding, with the dashing prince, blushing bride, and all that pomp and pageantry, that melts even the most cynical of hearts.

A bevy of beautiful young brides, including Catherine Middleton, Charlene Wittstock, Princess Victoria of Sweden, Tatiana Blatnik, Autumn Kelly, and Sophie Winkleman, have recently joined the royal fray and we are still clamoring for every detail of their storybook celebrations.

One only needs to look to Princess Grace and Princess Diana to see how royal brides can influence global fashion to an overwhelming extent. But these days, it's not only about what newly wedded royal women are wearing—it's more about what they are *doing*. Which charities are they supporting? Which causes are they championing? In the coming years, it will be interesting to see how these ladies use their new titles and royal connections to have a positive impact.

As the future Queen of Sweden, Princess Victoria's career is already laid out for her. But will Kate Middleton be able to fill the void that Princess Diana left behind? Will the new Princess Charlene be able to replace Grace Kelly as Monaco's female figurehead? Will Lady Frederick Windsor forge ahead with her acting career? Will Autumn return to her Asian studies once she bears the queen's first great-grandchild? Only time will tell. Although joining a royal house often means devoting all of your time to duty and tradition, these talented ladies are sure to shine in their own unique ways.

# HRH CATHERINE, DUCHESS OF CAMBRIDGE

**THE GROOM:** Second in line to the British throne, Prince William's parents are HRH Prince Charles and the late Diana, Princess of Wales. His fairy tale lineage and swoonful good looks once made William the most sought after bachelor in the world.

**THE BRIDE:** Born January 9, 1982, Kate Middleton attended Marlborough College before earning a degree in art history from St. Andrews University, where she met and began secretly dating Prince William. Known for her glossy chestnut hair, demure smile, levelheadedness, and perfectly polished fashion sense, Kate is extremely photogenic and entirely scandal-free, which made her ideal HRH material. Always immaculately turned out, Kate looks like she was born to be a Windsor. Her staples include tailored suits, jeans with boots and tweed jackets, wrap dresses, and Philip Treacy hats. (She is also leading the way when it comes to teaching England the value of a good, American-style blow-dry!)

Among Kate's many hobbies are photography, field hockey, tennis, and country pursuits like polo and horse racing. Before starting her official royal duties, Kate helped her parents with their highly successful business, Party Pieces, and once worked as an accessories buyer for UK fashion chain Jigsaw.

At first, Kate and William were just friends, and then housemates, but in 2003, their romance officially blossomed. The world was overjoyed when Kate's engagement to Prince William was announced in November 2010, making her the first non-blueblood since the 1600s to marry a future British monarch. We love Kate because she is poised, confident, and extremely family-oriented. Not only will she become the first Queen of England with a university degree, but she has shown the world that if you conduct yourself with the grace and dignity of a princess, your background is irrelevant.

**KATE'S CHARITIES:**

- ◆ *The Starlight Children's Foundation* Helps brighten the lives of seriously and terminally ill children by granting their wishes and providing hospital entertainment. A favorite cause of the Middleton family, Kate and William co-hosted a table at a recent black-tie benefit. http://www.starlight.org.uk/
- ◆ *Oxford's Children's Hospital* Kate recently attended an eighties-themed rollerskating disco in aid of the charity, which was set up in memory of her school friend Thomas Waley-Cohen, who tragically died of bone cancer at age twenty. http://www.oxfordradcliffe .nhs.uk/forpatients/departments/children/home.aspx
- ◆ *Place2be* Kate helped focus the limelight on this school-based counseling service dedicated to the emotional well-being of children, their families, and the whole school community. http://www.the place2be.org.uk/
- ◆ *Babes in Arms* Kate trained for a rowing challenge across the English Channel in aid of this charity that sponsors research into cot death and other abnormalities that affect newborn babies. http:// www.babes-in-arms.org/
- ◆ *CHASE Hospice for Children* Kate supports this charity in memory of England and Surrey cricketer Ben Hollioake, who was killed in a tragic car crash at age twenty-four. http://www.chasecare.org.uk/ page.asp?section=61&sectionTitle=CHASE+Ben+Hollioake+Fund
- ◆ *Raleigh International* A UK-based educational development charity that aims to help people of all backgrounds and nationalities to discover their full potential. Both Kate and Prince William are Raleigh alumni—Prince William went to Chile with Raleigh International in 2000, and Kate attended only a few months later in 2001. http://www.raleighinternational.org/

**THE ROYAL WEDDING**: The marriage of HRH Prince William of Wales to Miss Catherine Middleton took place at Westminster Abbey on Friday April 29, 2011, with an estimated television audience of two billion viewers—nearly a third of the planet!

After much speculation, Kate wore an ivory satin gown with full-length sleeves and intricate lace appliqué, heavily inspired by Princess Grace of Monaco, designed by Alexander McQueen, and customized by Sarah Burton. Her something borrowed was the Cartier Halo tiara, on loan from the queen. The aisle of the abbey was lined with real trees, and the pews were filled with nineteen hundred eminent guests from all over the world. After the ceremony, Kate and William (the new Duke and Duchess of Cambridge) stood upon the iconic balcony of Buckingham Palace and kissed in front of London's cheering crowds, before jumping into a vintage Aston Martin to wave to their well-wishers. Later that evening, Prince Charles hosted a black-tie wedding reception for three hundred of their closest friends and family, where the happy couple danced to "Your Song" by Elton John.

The newlyweds have requested that anyone wishing to send them a wedding gift consider donating to their charitable fund, which aids causes reflecting their personal passions and values. http://www.royalweddingcharityfund.org/

# HSH CHARLENE, PRINCESS OF MONACO

**THE GROOM:** Albert II, Sovereign Prince of Monaco, was born March 14, 1958. He is the head of the House of Grimaldi and the current ruler of the Principality of Monaco. He is the son of Rainier III, Prince of Monaco, and the American actress Grace Kelly.

Until recently, Albert had quite a playboy reputation. (His previous girlfriends included Claudia Schiffer, Naomi Campbell, and Brooke Shields.) The prince's fiftieth birthday came and went and he had yet to announce an engagement. Still, Monaco's royal succession did not depend on Albert choosing a princess. In fact, the constitution was changed to ensure that the Grimaldi throne would pass to Princess Caroline's children (Andrea, Charlotte, and Pierre) in the event that Albert remained a bachelor. Many even thought that young Andrea would beat his uncle Albert to the altar!

But royal watchers across the world rejoiced when Albert's betrothal to Charlene was finally announced in June 2010, bringing some much-needed stability to Monaco's royal family. The couple married in July 2011, bringing us a shiny new Princess of Monaco.

**THE BRIDE:** Charlene Wittstock was born January 25, 1978, in Rhodesia. This South African swimming champion and former model was first spotted with Prince Albert II of Monaco (twenty years her senior) at the opening ceremony of the 2006 Turin Winter Olympics. Charlene declares that the moment she met him she felt a profound sense of destiny.

Like Albert, Charlene is a serious sports aficionado—she loves to surf and hike, but most of all, she loves to swim. The statuesque blonde holds several national swimming awards in South Africa and swam in the Olympic relay team at the 2000 Sydney Games. Meanwhile, Prince Albert was part of Monaco's Olympic bobsled team for five consecutive years.

Prince Albert once declared, "The woman of my life will have to resemble my mother." When one's mother happens to be Hollywood goddess Grace Kelly, this is a formidable requirement! But tall, willowy Charlene (who wears her icy blond hair in the same chignon made famous by Princess Grace) certainly holds more than a passing resemblance. In glamorous evening dresses that show off her swimmer's physique, Charlene looks every inch a royal consort. It's no wonder Giorgio Armani chose her to be one of his style ambassadors.

**THE ROYAL WEDDING:** The last time Monaco celebrated the wedding of its ruling prince was in 1956, when Prince Albert's father married Grace Kelly—quite an act to follow! But Monaco, with its usual splendor, did not let us down. On the eve of the wedding, a celebratory concert by the Eagles was offered to all Monegasque citizens. On July 1, 2011, the couple's civil ceremony was held in the opulent Throne Room of the Grimaldi Palace. Their religious ceremony was held the following day in the palace's main courtyard. Charlene looked radiant in a white Armani dress and a diamond hair ornament on loan from Princess Caroline. Afterward, in line with an ancient tradition, Charlene lay down her bridal bouquet in the Church of St. Dévote to honor the patron saint of Monaco. The official dinner was prepared by three-star French chef Alain Ducasse and followed by a magnificent fireworks display for the whole country to enjoy.

**QUOTE:** "I'm in a unique position where I can make a big difference. My hope is to harness the tremendous resources Monaco possesses to address a multitude of global problems."[11]

**CHARLENE'S CHARITIES:**
◆ *Nelson Mandela Day* Close to the man himself, Charlene was deeply involved in the annual event dedicated to Mandela's life's work and charitable organizations. http://en.mandeladay.com/Home.aspx

- *The World Wildlife Fund* Strives to protect endangered wildlife, tackle climate change, and promote sustainable use of resources. Charlene once wore a fabulous evening gown with a large WWF panda logo emblazoned on its skirts. http://www.wwf.org/
- *The Princess Grace Foundation* Created by Prince Albert's mother, this charity supports pediatric medicine and humanitarian aid for handicapped children. Charlene also champions the *Special Olympics of Monaco*. http://www.fondation-psse-grace.mc/frameseteng.html/
- *The Monaco Red Cross* Aims to protect the lives and dignity of victims of war and internal violence and to provide them with assistance. Prince Albert is president. http://www.icrc.org/
- *The Born Free Foundation* An international wildlife charity working to prevent cruelty and alleviate suffering. http://www.bornfree.org.uk/
- *The Prince Albert II of Monaco Foundation* Created by Albert in 2006, the foundation seeks to protect the environment and encourage sustainable development. http://www.fpa2.mc/default.asp?lang=en
- *Fight Aids Monaco* Founded by Albert's sister, HSH Princess Stephanie, this charity promotes awareness of the danger still posed by HIV/AIDS. http://www.fightaidsmonaco.com/accueil-eng.html/

# CROWN PRINCESS VICTORIA OF SWEDEN

**THE BRIDE:** Born July 14, 1977, Victoria is the eldest of King Carl XVI Gustaf and Queen Silvia's three children. Because Sweden is the first monarchy to allow the eldest child to inherit the throne regardless of gender, Victoria is destined to become Sweden's future queen. As things stand, she is the only female heir-apparent in the world. Victoria speaks four languages and is known for her fervent interest in diplomacy and international relations.

**THE GROOM:** Daniel Westling (now known as Prince Daniel, Duke of Västergötland) was born in Sweden on September 15, 1973. Before his marriage to Princess Victoria, Daniel worked as her personal trainer. Daniel's working relationship with the sweet-natured princess quickly blossomed into an eight-year romance. Daniel eventually opened a fitness company called Balance Training, with three gyms in central Stockholm. But upon receiving the title of prince, he stepped down as CEO of the company.

**THE ROYAL WEDDING:** Their wedding was held at Stockholm Cathedral on June 19, 2010—the thirty-fourth wedding anniversary of the King and Queen of Sweden. Victoria wore an ivory-colored gown of duchess satin, with a five-meter train, designed by Swedish dressmaker Par Engshed. Her antique lace veil was held in place by the same cameo tiara that was worn by Victoria's mother, Queen Silvia, at her marriage in 1975. The wedding was attended by twelve hundred guests from around the world, including six kings and nine queens. After the ceremony, the happy couple boarded the royal barge to the reception at Drottningholm Palace. Following a wedding feast of lobster, caviar, and champagne, Princess Victoria and her new prince took to the dance floor, where they executed a perfect waltz. So romantic!

# PRINCESS TATIANA OF GREECE AND DENMARK

**THE GROOM:** Prince Nikolaos of Greece and Denmark (born October 1, 1969) is the second son of King Constantine of Greece and the elder brother of the aforementioned eligible royals Prince Philippos and Princess Theodora. The nephew of two Queens—Queen Margrethe II of Denmark is his mother's sister; Queen Sofia of Spain is his father's sister—Nikolaos has dozens of royal cousins throughout Europe. Prince Nikolaos graduated from Brown University with an BA in International Relations and works for his father's London office.

**THE BRIDE:** Venezuelan born Tatiana Blatnik is the granddaughter of Countess Ellinka von Ensiedel of Dresden. The Grace Kelly look-alike attended school in Switzerland and later studied Sociology at Georgetown University in the U.S. before working as a PR and events manager for fashion designer Diane von Furstenberg. She had been quietly dating Prince Nikolaos for six years before their engagement was officially announced.

**THE ROYAL WEDDING:** On August 25, 2010, Tatiana and Nikolaos wed in a lavish sunset wedding on the beautiful Greek island of Spetses. Throngs of royals from across Europe gathered for the ceremony at the Church of Saint Nicholas. As a ravishing blonde with regal heritage, Tatiana looked every bit like a fairy tale princess on her wedding day. She arrived in a traditional horse-drawn carriage wearing a full-length strapless ivory gown with lace overlay by Venezuelan designer Angel Sanchez. It was worn with a full-length veil, matching lace bolero jacket, and a dazzling diamond tiara borrowed from her new mother-in-law, Queen Anne Marie. (The tiara was also worn at the wedding of Tatiana's sister-in-law, Princess Marie-Chantal.) Tatiana is now known as HRH Princess Nikolaos of Greece and Denmark. The newlyweds reside in London.

**FAVORITE CHARITY:**

◆ *The Anna-Maria Foundation* Provides aid to people who have suffered due to natural disasters. Nikolaos is a board member. http://www.greekroyalfamily.gr/index.cfm?get=foundation

# LADY FREDERICK WINDSOR

**THE GROOM:** Born April 6, 1979, Lord Frederick Windsor is the son of Prince and Princess Michael of Kent and is thirty-seventh in line to the British throne. His father is a first cousin of HM Queen Elizabeth II; his sister is the aforementioned Lady Gabriella Windsor. Educated at Eton College, "Freddie" later graduated from Oxford University with a degree in Classics. He now works for investment bank J.P. Morgan and recently transferred to their California offices so he could be with his wife as she pursues her acting career. The romantic aristocrat proposed to his bride-to-be on Valentine's Day.

**THE BRIDE:** Sophie Lara Winkleman was born in London on August 5, 1980. Her father is a prominent publisher and her mother is a copywriter and author. Her half sister is TV anchor Claudia Winkleman. Sophie studied English Literature at Cambridge University, where she joined the famed dramatic society Cambridge Footlights, which launched her successful acting career. After several roles for UK television, Sophie filmed an American comedy series entitled *100 Questions for Charlotte Payne* and is now working on a new historical series about the *Titanic* where she will play the American silent-movie star Dorothy Gibson.

**THE ROYAL WEDDING:** Sophie and Freddie married on September 12, 2009, in a society wedding at Hampton Court Palace, which was attended by several young royals, including Princess Eugenie of York. The beautiful bride arrived in a silver Rolls-Royce, wearing a white silk beaded gown, with a three-meter train, designed by Anna Bystrova from Roza Couture. The service was held in the sumptuous Chapel Royal and was followed by a reception of champagne, canapés, and cake in the magnificent Great Hall. Celebrations continued with a dinner and dance at the London home of the groom's godmother, Lady Annabel Goldsmith. The newlyweds currently reside in Los Angeles, California.

# AUTUMN PHILLIPS

**THE GROOM:** Born November 15, 1977, Peter Phillips is the son of the Princess Royal and Captain Mark Phillips and the oldest grandchild of HM Queen Elizabeth II. His godfather is the Prince of Wales and his younger sister is the aforementioned Zara Phillips. Peter is eleventh in line to succeed to the British throne. He graduated from the University of Exeter with a degree in sports science.

**THE BRIDE:** Autumn Patricia Kelly was born May 3, 1978, in Quebec. The pretty Canadian graduated from McGill University with a degree in East Asian studies. She met her handsome husband-to-be during the 2003 Montreal Grand Prix, where she was working in the BMW hospitality tent. Their engagement was announced in July 2007.

**THE ROYAL WEDDING:** The marriage took place in Windsor Castle's St. George's Chapel on May 17, 2008. The entire wedding was covered extensively in a special edition of *Hello!* magazine. Autumn wore an ivory duchess satin wedding gown by Sassi Holford with a cathedral train, a lace bolero, and a diamond tiara on loan from her mother-in-law, Princess Anne. Attended by most senior members of the British royal family, the lavish reception was held at Frogmore House. The couple resides in Hong Kong, and on December 29, 2010, Autumn gave birth to the queen's first great-grandchild—a baby girl named Savannah.

# POWER COUPLES

*A*fter all the pomp and pageantry of a regal wedding is behind them, young royal romances eventually blossom into hardworking royal families. Royal couples must learn to juggle sovereign duties, parenthood, and the media spotlight and to do so with grace, dignity, and a constant smile.

Here we look at the crown princes and princesses of the Netherlands, Belgium, and Greece, as well as their gorgeous royal children. In their official portraits, all appear picture-perfect, with happy smiles and sunny complexions, but raising a royal family can be hard work. Not only must they successfully maintain their own royal duties, but they must raise the next generation of royals and see to it that the right values are instilled within them.

A life of extreme privilege can often breed disaster in adulthood, so these royal parents work hard to demonstrate the importance of charity and an entrepreneurial spirit. Crown Princess Marie-Chantal, who started a successful children's clothing company all on her own, is a great role model for her five children. Prince Willem-Alexander,

Crown Princess Maxima, Crown Prince Philippe, and Crown Princess Mathilde all strive to relax the ceremonial pomp and circumstance of their positions so their children can have a down-to-earth upbringing and remain as normal as possible.

Without exception, the young royal families of the Netherlands, Belgium, and Greece are using their royal titles for the greater good, with a huge array of philanthropic commitments. Yet through it all Maxima, Mathilde, and Marie-Chantal still make the time to take their children to school each day just like any regular loving parent would. Surrounded by such fantastic role models and raised in such a loving environment, we can be sure that the next generation of princes and princesses will make us proud.

**PRECEDING PAGE:**

Dutch Royals Crown Prince Willem-Alexander and wife Crown Princess Maxima with their daughters Princess Alexia, Princess Ariane, and Princess Catharina-Amalia

**ABOVE:**

Crown Prince Willem-Alexander with Princess Ariane and Princess Catharina-Amalia, and Crown Princess Maxima with Princess Alexia

# HRH WILLEM-ALEXANDER, PRINCE OF ORANGE, AND HRH CROWN PRINCESS MAXIMA OF THE NETHERLANDS

**THE PRINCE:** Born April 27, 1967, Prince Willem-Alexander is the oldest child of Queen Beatrix of the Netherlands. The tall, blond prince is first in line to inherit the Dutch throne and is a direct descendant of the British King George II.

Queen Beatrix insisted that her children have a normal upbringing and told others to call her son by his first name rather than his title until he was sixteen. She also made sure that Willem-Alexander was educated in local grammar schools, where he could mix with children from all social backgrounds. As a result, the prince is extremely down-to-earth.

The prince enjoys running, tennis, skiing, sailing, golf, rock climbing, horseback riding, and diving, but his greatest love is flying. Since gaining his military pilot's licence, the prince has flown humanitarian relief missions in Kenya and has worked as a pilot for Dutch government officials.

In 1999, Willem-Alexander met a striking Argentinean blonde named Maxima at party in Seville. He was instantly taken by Maxima's winning smile and unassuming nature and crossed the Atlantic one month later in order to visit her. They announced their engagement in 2001.

**THE PRINCESS:** Princess Maxima was born in Buenos Aires, Argentina, on May 17, 1971, as Maxima Zorreguieta. She was working for

Deutsche Bank in New York City when she started dating Willem-Alexander. The couple married in royal style on February 2, 2002, making Prince Willem-Alexander the first male heir to the Dutch throne to marry in the Netherlands. (Willem I, II, and III married in the native countries of their brides.)

Maxima now represents the Dutch Royal House at official occasions of all kinds and accompanies the queen on state visits.

**THEIR ROYAL OFFSPRING:** The proud prince and princess have three beautiful daughters: HRH Princess Catharina-Amalia (born December 7, 2003), HRH Princess Alexia (born June 26, 2005), and HRH Princess Ariane (born April 10, 2007).

**USING THEIR TITLES FOR THE GREATER GOOD:** The Prince of Orange has a strong passion for ethical water management and believes that solving problems related to water access and sanitation will play a central role in eradicating poverty. The prince is an honorary member of the World Commission on Water for the 21st Century and chair of the Water Advisory Committee in the Netherlands. He also chairs the UN's Advisory Board on Water and Sanitation, which contributes to solving water-related problems all over the world.

Prince Willem-Alexander is also a patron of the Global Water Partnership, which supports the sustainable development and management of water resources at all levels. http://www.gwp.org/

Meanwhile, Princess Maxima feels passionately about the integration of immigrants into Dutch culture and stresses the importance of learning the Dutch language—as she did upon her engagement—in order to fully participate in Dutch society. Her Royal Highness also works as patroness to Scouting Nederland, the Royal Orchestra Foundation, the Royal Tropical Institute, and the Royal Institute for Culture and Language.

Most recently, the princess has been busy promoting the importance of "inclusive finance" to reduce poverty and due to her expertise in the field, she has been named the UN special advocate for inclusive finance for development.

Finally, both Princess Maxima and Prince Willem-Alexander are patrons of the Orange Fund, which promotes social welfare and cohesion in the Netherlands. The royal couple regularly visit projects supported by the Orange Fund, and every year, Princess Maxima presents *Appeltje van Oranje* awards to institutions that set an example in the field of welfare. http://www.oranjefonds.nl/

# CROWN PRINCE PHILIPPE AND CROWN PRINCESS MATHILDE OF BELGIUM

**THE PRINCE:** Born in Brussels on April 15, 1960, Crown Prince Philippe is the son of King Albert II and Queen Paola of Belgium. He studied Constitutional History at Oxford before completing a master's degree in Political Science at Stanford University in California. Some thought he might remain a bachelor forever, but just before he turned forty, the prince gave the Belgian people their longed-for princess. He married Mathilde on December 4, 1999 (the marriage ceremony was repeated in three languages), in what became the last royal wedding of the twentieth century.

**THE PRINCESS:** The glamorous Mathilde was born on January 20, 1973, the daughter of the Count and Countess Patrick d'Udekem d'Acoz. The intelligent, down-to-earth aristocrat studied Psychology and was working as a speech therapist in her own practice when she met Prince Philippe during a game of tennis. Because she was raised in the French part of the country yet hails from a noble Flemish family, Princess Mathilde was welcomed by both sides of Belgium. She's fluent in Dutch, French, English, and Italian, and when Philippe becomes king, Mathilde will be the country's first ever Belgian-born queen consort.

**THEIR ROYAL OFFSPRING:** The crown prince and crown princess have been blessed with two sons and two daughters: Princess Elisabeth (Belgium's future queen, born October 25, 2001); Prince Gabriel (born August 20, 2003); Prince Emmanuel (born October 4, 2005), and Princess Eléonore (born April 16, 2008).

**USING THEIR TITLES FOR THE GREATER GOOD:** Prince Philippe created the Prince Philippe Fund in 1998 with the aim of fostering dialogue between the different cultural communities of Belgium through educational and professional exchange programs. Prince Philippe also acts as honorary chairman of the Belgian Federal Council for Sustainable Development, which supports research into energy, climate, and biodiversity.

Meanwhile, Princess Mathilde is very concerned about the plight of vulnerable people, particularly children, and as a result she set up the Princess Mathilde Fund in December 2000. Each year the fund awards prizes to laudable projects that help improve the situations of children at risk.

In addition, Princess Mathilde is patron to several associations that work to help vulnerable women and improve education. In conjunction with UNICEF, the princess has presided over several humanitarian missions abroad, promoting the importance of children's rights, health, the empowerment of women, poverty eradication, and good governance. She has also worked as a United Nations envoy for the International Year on Micro-credit and as a UNICEF special representative for their campaign to help children orphaned by HIV/AIDS.

PRECEDING PAGE:

Crown Prince Pavlos and Crown Princess Marie-Chantal with children, Princess Maria Olympia, Prince Constantine Alexios, Prince Achileas-Andreas, Prince Odysseas-Kimon, and Prince Aristidis-Stavros

ABOVE:

Prince Pavlos holding son Prince Aristidos-Stavros, Princess Marie-Chantal, Princess Maria-Olympia, Prince Achileas-Andreas, Prince Constantine Alexios, and Prince Odysseas-Kimon

# CROWN PRINCE PAVLOS AND CROWN PRINCESS MARIE-CHANTAL OF GREECE

**THE PRINCE:** Born May 20, 1967, Crown Prince Pavlos is the eldest son of King Constantine II. If Constantine were ever restored to the throne, Pavlos would be his heir apparent. Prince Pavlos is also the highest ranking person in the British line of succession to be triply related to Queen Victoria.

Pavlos was educated in London, at the Hellenic College, before training at the UK's Sandhurst military academy. Later he attended Georgetown University in Washington, DC, where he completed a master's degree in foreign service and shared an apartment with his cousin, Prince Felipe of Spain.

The crown prince met the stunning American heiress Marie-Chantal on a blind date at a friend's dinner party, and later proposed to her on a snowy ski lift in Gstaad. Pavlos was one of the first European princes of his generation to marry a commoner, starting a trend that the princes of Norway, Spain, and Denmark would soon follow.

**THE PRINCESS:** Marie-Chantal Claire Miller was born September 17, 1968, to an American father and a South American mother. The delicate blond socialite grew up in Hong Kong and went to school in Switzerland and New York before fate brought her and Prince Pavlos together at a friend's dinner party. She declares that when she was seated next to the handsome Greek royal, it was "love at first sight."

Her wedding to Prince Pavlos brought together the largest group of royals in London since Queen Elizabeth married Prince Philip in

1947. Today, Pavlos and Marie-Chantal are known as one of the most popular and glamorous couples in international society.

Celebrated for her elegant fashion sense, Marie-Chantal successfully launched a line of luxury children's clothing that is sold in London, New York, and Greece. http://www.mariechantal.com

**THEIR ROYAL OFFSPRING:** The prince and princess are proud parents to five bouncy blond children with traditional Greek names: Maria-Olympia (born 1996), Constantine Alexios (born 1998), Achileas-Andreas (born 2000), Odysseas-Kimon (born 2004), and Aristidis-Stavros (born 2008).

**USING THEIR TITLES FOR THE GREATER GOOD:** Crown Prince Pavlos is the U.S. committee chairman of United World Colleges and sits on the board of the New York City Ballet.

Along with his three siblings (the aforementioned Prince Nikolaos, Prince Philippos, and Princess Theodora), Prince Pavlos is an acting board member of The Anna-Maria Foundation, which provides aid to people who have suffered due to natural disasters. http://www.greek royalfamily.gr/index.cfm?get=foundation

Crown Princess Marie-Chantal sits on the board of the New York School of American Ballet and the Animal Medical Centre, and is a founding member of the Board of Venetian Heritage. She is also a trustee for London's Royal Academy.

Pavlos and Marie-Chantal cochair the U.S. Committee for World in Harmony—a nonprofit founded by the prince's aunt, Princess Irene of Greece and Denmark, to provide humanitarian assistance to those who need it most. http://www.worldinharmony.org/index_en.html

# THE BRIGHTEST, YOUNGEST QUEEN

*H*er Majesty Rania Al-Abdullah is the world's youngest living queen. She is also the most stylish and the most in touch with the youth of today—both within her own country of Jordan and throughout the world.

Queen Rania twitters (@QueenRania). She's even on Facebook and YouTube. And when it comes to humanitarianism, no royal can beat her—for the glamorous Queen Rania is just as famous for her progressive philanthropy as she is for her supermodel looks.

Her designer wardrobe may be immaculate, but Queen Rania has made it clear to her fans that she is more than a royal fashion icon. She is a businesswoman, an activist, a mother, and a wife—and she is vehemently committed to making the world a better place for women and children.

Queen Rania has thrown herself into full-time charity work with a creative gusto that hasn't been seen since the late Princess Diana of Wales. She has become a world-renowned role model for women, a global advocate for education, and a strong supporter of social development. Her philanthropic activities encompass community empowerment, economic fairness, women's rights, and the environment, among other issues. As an official advocate for UNICEF and honorary chairperson for UNGEI, she campaigns tirelessly on behalf of all children in need. Most importantly, as an Arab Muslim woman, Queen Rania is committed to reconciling people of different faiths and encouraging cross-cultural dialogue, particularly among young people. (And yet somehow, she still finds time to bake chocolate chip cookies for her four children!)

There is no doubt that Queen Rania of Jordan is one of the most intriguing women on the planet. But she is also a working mother who is dedicated to changing the world—and in that way, she is a thoroughly modern monarch, one whom we should all aspire to become more like—with or without a royal kingdom.

# QUEEN RANIA OF JORDAN

**HIM:** Abdullah became King of Jordan on February 7, 1999, upon the death of his father, King Hussein. Since his ascension to the throne, King Abdullah II has continued his late father's commitment to creating a strong and positive moderating role for Jordan within the Arab world.

**HER:** Born in Kuwait on August 31, 1970, Rania received a thoroughly Western education and ultimately earned a degree in business administration from the American University in Cairo. Upon graduation, her career path led her to high-powered roles at Citibank and Apple Computer. Despite her killer heels and glossy hair, make no mistake: this queen is as brainy as she is beautiful.

**REGAL ROMANCE:** Abdullah and Rania met at a dinner party in 1993 and it was love at first sight. They were married just five months later, and in 1999, Rania became the world's youngest living queen at just twenty-nine years old. The royal couple are still considered to be a perfect intellectual match and are said to always be on the same wavelength when it comes to humanitarian issues.

**HEIR AND SPARES:** Crown Prince Hussein (born June 28, 1994), Princess Iman (born September 27, 1996), Princess Salma (born September 26, 2000), Prince Hashem (born January 30, 2005).

**QUOTE:** "At the end of the day you are living your life for the people that you represent. It's an honor and a privilege to have that chance to make a difference—a qualitative difference in people's lives—and it's my responsibility to make the most out of that opportunity."[12]

**PHILANTHROPY:** Queen Rania has pushed for education reform, is an enthusiastic supporter of the micro-fund movement, and continues to discuss formerly taboo topics like domestic violence, child abuse, and honor killings. She believes that there is a direct relationship between increasing education and eliminating poverty, and feels that many problems (including terrorism) stem from intolerance. Because of this, Rania has purposely set out to create more educational and economic opportunities for young people and to encourage more cross-cultural dialogue.

QUOTE: "No matter where we come from, what we look like, how we dress, or to whom we pray, when it comes to what makes us laugh or cry, when it comes to what we dream of for ourselves and for our children, when it comes to how hard we work each day, we are usually more alike than we are different."[13]

**QUEEN RANIA'S CHARITIES:**

◆ *The Jordan River Foundation* Chaired by Queen Rania, the foundation aims to empower society, especially women and children, in order to improve quality of life and to secure a better future for all Jordanians. http://www.jordanriver.jo/

◆ *Madrasati* Another of Queen Rania's initiatives, this charity brings together businesses, non-governmental organizations, and communities to rejuvenate schools in need. http://www.madrasati.jo/site.html

◆ *The Queen Rania Teacher Academy* Advances education in Jordan and throughout the Middle East by providing teachers with access to training, professional support, and the latest research on educational methods. http://www.qrta.edu.jo/

◆ *The Children's Museum of Jordan* A nonprofit organization launched by Queen Rania in 2007 to encourage and nurture lifelong learning in children and their families. http://www.cmj.jo/hmq_letter

# EVER AFTER

*"We've been brought up in different times.*
*The world is changing, as everyone knows.*
*We've changed with it."*

**—PRINCE HARRY**

The world's few remaining royal families are living relics from another age. While it was once widely believed that monarchs were descended from the gods or divinely anointed, in this new millennium, it is clear that our beloved bluebloods are all too mortal.

Young, rich, and beautiful, these youngsters realize that being born into royalty has its perks, but they are also acutely aware that being royal means living life in a fishbowl. While the generation before them struggled to come to terms with their royal position in this modern, media-driven age, it appears that these young royals are effortlessly thriving in the new status quo.

Tragically, iconic royals like Diana, Princess of Wales, and Princess Grace of Monaco are no longer with us. But their lives remain the subject of intense global fascination—and so, too, the lives of their offspring.

The Monegasque children seem to have been born with elegance in their DNA and have put Monaco back on the map as one of

Europe's most glamorous and youthful monarchies. Meanwhile, Prince William and Prince Harry have not only kept their mother's flame alight, but have captured the adoration of millions. (And with the addition of Catherine Middleton, it's safe to say that William's glamour has increased tenfold.) All of the young aristocrats and royals mentioned in this book have a strong sense duty, a unique sense of fun, and a fresh determination to leave their own mark on the monarchy. But will they avoid the mistakes of their parents?

Whatever the future holds, we know that in this ever-changing world, these bright young bluebloods will continue to pique our interest, surprise the media, shock their families, pull our heartstrings, and honor their historical royal heritage—while inspiring everyone to find the human nobility that dwells inside us all.

# ACKNOWLEDGMENTS

Special thanks to my agent, Laura Langlie (for having enough faith in me to send a glass slipper); to my editor, Kate Seaver (for recognizing that she's not the only one who wants to know where Prince Harry hangs out!); and to Giulia Carnera Secchi (for her fantastic photo editing.) I would also like to thank my wonderful, indulgent husband, who doesn't seem to mind that I spend most of my time researching eligible princes.

# SOURCES

1 *Hello!* magazine, February 22, 2010
2 *Tatler*, September 2005
3 hellomagazine.com
4 AP, 2003
5 *Tatler*, 2009
6 Translated from Swedish *Elle*, January 2010
7 *Vanity Fair*, June 2009
8 *Vanity Fair*, June 2009
9 hellomagazine.com
10 hellomagazine.com
11 *Tatler*, December 2010
12 http://www.queenrania.jo
13 http://www.queenrania.jo

# PHOTO CREDITS